SKate LEGENDS

Michael Brooke

ᴀɴ**Othe**r book by Michael Brooke:
The Concrete Wave: The History of Skateboarding

Copyright © 2002 by Michael Brooke

Published in 2002 by Olmstead Press: Milford, Connecticut

ISBN: 1 894622-22-7

Editorial Sales Rights and Permission Inquiries should be addressed to:
Olmstead Press, 22 Broad Street, Suite 34, Milford, CT 06460
Email: Editor@lpcgroup.com

Manufactured in the United States of America
1 3 5 7 9 10 8 6 4 2

Cover and Book Design: Clint Rogerson

Front Cover Photos: **Mickey Maga, Tony Alva, Tony Hawk, Jamie Thomas**
Back Cover Photo: **Jay Adams**

Printed and bound in Canada

Contents

DAEWON SONG

Introducti on

In an earlier book, The Concrete Wave, I documented the history of skateboarding primarily through manufacturers. It's been over two and half years since the book arrived, and to say that it has had a profound effect on my life would be an understatement. The success of the book spawned both a magazine and a television series. Based on the success of The Concrete Wave, I have been given another chance to create a new book — something that I am most grateful for.

The book you are now holding showcases the history of skateboarding through some of its legendary riders. These are the pioneers, the skate stars who stand out from the crowd. They're the people who dedicate long hours perfecting a trick. Through their ingenuity and talent, they take skateboarding to a new level.

These skate legends possess a passion for skateboarding that is extremely deep. In my opinion, they represent the true soul of skateboarding — they stick with it through the ups and downs. These skateboarders could be from your neighborhood, your local skatepark or your state or province. Wherever they're from, these skate legends keep the spirit of skateboarding alive.

Each era of skateboarding has produced literally thousands of incredibly talented riders. Suffice to say, there is no way I could have fit all of these skaters into one hundred and sixty pages. While there will most likely be a huge outcry regarding some of the skaters not included in this book, this in no way should take away from their legendary status. We just didn't have the space.

In terms of the 150 profiles found in this book you will find a wide range of information. Some legends are famous for what they do; others are famous for what they are or what they've achieved. There are a number of skate legends that are featured in many magazines and videos, others shun the spotlight. Whatever the case, these 150 profiles illustrate the best of what skateboarding has to offer.

I hope that older skaters enjoy the nostalgic look back at the past and that today's new generation of skaters get a good sense of just how far skateboarding has progressed. If you'd like to comment on the book, I would love to hear from you. Email me at mbrooke@interlog.com.

Michael Brooke
Winter 2001

Thank You

As this book spans four generations of skate legends, it would have been impossible to write it completely by myself. I am grateful to Dale Smith for his work on the 60s legends. Perry Gladstone and Bill Danforth were very helpful in navigating the 80s. Evan Cousans, Dave Buchanan and Elliot Rudner assisted with the 90s legends. Norm MacDonald's encyclopedic knowledge of skateboarding was also of great help.

I am also appreciative of the many photographers and skate companies who have helped with the photos in this book. These include Jim Goodrich, Lynn Cooper, Scott Starr, Glen Miyoda, Miki Vuckovich, Scott Serfas, Brandon Sohar and many more.

I am grateful to Nick Pitt and Jim Williamson of Warwick Publishing who had faith in my first book and allowed me to create a second. Warwick's graphic designer Clint Rogerson and copy editor Melinda Tate have worked hard on this book and I am privileged to work with them. A final publishing industry thank-you to David Wilk at LPC Group for his encouragement.

A big thank-you to my parents who have always supported my love of skateboarding. They stick by me even when I get kicked out of skate spots by security guards. To my wife Michal and children Maya, Jonathan and Ethan, thanks for putting up with the long hours of writing, the road rash, wobbly knees and general mayhem that I cause.

Finally, I want to acknowledge all of the skate legends found in this book and those, who for reasons of space, didn't make it. Thank you for your dedication to skateboarding. There are millions of skaters around the world (myself included) who are grateful for your skills and passion.

STEVE CABALLERO

Skateboarding's roots lie within surf culture. When the surf was flat, ingenious kids dismantled rollerskates and nailed them to a 2x4. As the popularity of surf culture exploded, so did skateboarding. By 1963, there were thousands of skateboards being sold each day. The technology found in the first wave of skateboarding was quite primitive. The wheels were made from steel or clay and the trucks were very basic. Despite these limitations, the early skate legends were able to establish themselves with a style and ingenuity that would pave the way for future generations.

Skaters practiced hours on tricks like nose wheelies, high jumps and handstands. Slalom skating got its start in the 1960s and some brave souls even tried their luck in empty backyard swimming pools. Bank riding was also developed at legendary spots like Paul Revere and Kenter elementary schools. While most skateboarders were content to cruise down the street, these skate legends took things to a whole new level.

Despite the explosive growth of skateboarding, it was obvious to many that the skateboards themselves were quite limiting. Clay wheels provided a very messy ride. The wheels couldn't grip the road and a small stone could send a skater flying. As a result of their unsafe design, many towns banned skateboarding and the industry evaporated quickly. However, in a few areas of the country (mainly southern California) a select number of people still kept skating. These people would help sow the seeds of the next wave of skateboarding.

Danny Bearer

Danny was a roller skater before he became a skateboarder. After seeing some guys using skateboards at the roller rink, Danny went home and took apart his roller skates to make his own skateboard.

Danny quickly mastered the board, taking first place in the National Championship at the 1964 Santa Monica Surf Fair Contest and First Place in the Double A Flatland Slalom at the International Skateboard Championships in 1965. Danny is known as one of the early bank riders. Some of his favorite spots were Paul Revere, Markey's and Belagio schools. He also enjoyed riding and touring the United States for the Hobie Skateboard Company.

Brad "Squeak" Bla[

Brad Blank took first place in the 1964 Anaheim Nationals — the first national skateboard contest ever held. He toured extensively with Makaha and influenced a great many skaters.

Harry "Skip" Frye

Skip Frye began surfing in 1958 and five years later took up skateboarding on a homemade board. In 1964 Skip's original plywood model was modified with fiberglass from a board factory to give it more strength and flex.

Skip had his own skate club called the Weavers. The Weavers were his surf buddies — Willie Phillips, Mike Hynson and Vince Turner. They rode the hills of Pacific Beach and a parking lot called the Concourse in downtown San Diego.

Skip was instrumental in assisting with the development of the FiberFlex skateboard from Gordon and Smith. The boards were specially designed to provide strength and flexibility. They allowed Skip and the Weaver Team, now known as the Gordon and Smith Skateboard Team, to excel in slalom skating. The team

competed in the 1965 First International Skateboard Championship. Willie and Skip gave a one–two punch in the slalom event — Willie took first and Skip got second.

For most of the 1960s and early 70s, Skip stayed within the world of surfing — competing and shaping boards. In the mid-1970s Skip got back into skateboarding when the urethane wheel came out. Skip spent countless hours riding the hills of La Costa, influencing a new generation of skaters like Henry Hester, Chris Yandell, Bob Scholberg and Denis Shufeldt.

Dave and Steve Hilton

Dave and Steve were southern Californians whose father played an important role in the development of the Hobie Super Surfer/Vita-Pakt Skateboard Company. Vita-Pakt was an orange juice product. The skateboard team tour was seen as a way to promote both Hilton's Citrus Fruit Company and the Hobie Skateboard line across the United States.

Dave was the first person to be featured on the cover of the Quarterly SkateBoarder magazine in 1964. Both Hilton boys performed numerous demos and competed in many contests. Steve took fifth place and Dave grabbed third place in the AA Division 1965 International Skateboard Championships. Dave and Steve were also featured in a Bruce Brown short film featuring the Hobie Skateboard Team.

the quarterly SKATEBOARDER

VOL. 1   NO. 1   WINTER / 50 CENTS

THE BIG JUMP — PERFORMANCE PLUS — SURF/ SKI / SKATEBOARD — NIGHT RALLIES

Mike Hynson

Mike is probably best known for his surfer image in the world-famous Bruce Brown movie, The Endless Summer. In the film, Mike and fellow surfer Robert August travel the world in search of the perfect wave. Mike was the second professional surfer to provide the surfer image to the Makaha Skateboard Company.

The Makaha Skateboard line advertisement in Surf Guide magazine stated that Makaha's boards were designed by surfing experts. Mike was a perfect fit for Makaha, as he was both a top surfer and a good skateboarder.

Mike rode with Skip Frye in the Weaver Skate Club in San Diego. Later on he traveled to Laguna Beach to skate the slalom courses with the Hobie team. In 1965 he and Skip Frye and the Weaver Skate Club became the Gordon and Smith Fiber Flex Skate Team.

Phil Edwards

Phil began surfing in 1946 when he moved from Long Beach to Oceanside, California. He is considered by many to be one of the world's greatest surfers. Phil's main interest is surfing and he has spent many years developing his own style of board. His surfboards have been in great demand since the 1950s.

In April of 1963, Phil and Hobie Alter, of Hobie Surfboards, worked together to create the first signature model surfboard for expert surfers. Besides having the first signature model, he was the first person to ride the Bonsai Pipeline. Phil also won the first Annual Surfer Poll Award along with countless other awards.

Phil's fame and popularity led him to Larry Stevenson of Makaha Skateboards. The two designed and produced the Phil Edwards Model and it quickly became a best seller. This model was designed for smooth and quick maneuverability to match Phil's graceful and stylish turning ability.

Without a doubt, Phil was a key component in launching skateboarding's first wave of popularity. In today's collectable skateboard market, the Phil Edwards Model is one of the most sought-after items.

Brandon "Woody" Woodward

Woody was born in Japan in 1954 and grew up on the beach in Malibu. He began surfing at age seven. A year later he picked up skateboarding.

Woody and his friends formed a skate team called the Bombers Surf and Skate Club. They had secret skating spots. One was behind a housing development that had a long and smooth hill. Another spot they called "The Maze" was located on J. Paul Getty's Malibu estate. They rode between the orange groves and the caged lions and tigers on the property.

Woody's style was influenced by top surfers Phil Edwards and Mike Doyle. He began riding for the Makaha Skateboard Team and in 1965 entered the International Skateboard Championship in Anaheim, California. He won in all events for his under-12 division. This included Flatland Slalom, Figure Eight and Tricks. After this, Woody moved on to skate for the Hobie Skateboard Team and took part in demonstrations across the U.S.

In the 1970s, Woody began skating for the Logan Earth Ski Team. Over a decade earlier, he had ridden with Bruce Logan on the Makaha team. It was while on this team that Woody took first place in the high jump at the Cow Palace in San Francisco.

Torger Johnson

Torger Johnson was a legend in both the 1960s and 70s. He invented many freestyle tricks, including the "space walk." Torger influenced a number of key skaters, including Bruce Logan and Tony Alva. Like many of his contemporaries, Torger had a very strong surfing background. Tragically, Torger died in 1988 in an automobile accident in Hawaii.

Johnson

Pat saw her first skateboard at the 1963 Hollywood Teen Fair. She was hired by a sporting goods store to give away skateboards at promotional events. When Pat had to stand in for a skateboard demonstrator one night, she ably performed a kickturn for the crowd.

Soon after, Pat joined the Hobie Skateboard Team and began traveling around the U.S. Pat and her brother were on the Hobie Skateboard Team at this time. In 1964 she won first place in the girls' division of the National Skateboard Championship at the Santa Monica Surf Fair.

Not only was Pat a competitive skateboarder but she also was quite a surfer. Growing up in San Diego her favorite surf spots were La Jolla, the Shores and Windandsea. Pat felt there was a definite connection between skateboarding and surfing.

Pat appeared on the cover of Life magazine (May 14, 1965), as well as on several television shows including the Tonight Show (with Johnny Carson). As a professional skater, Pat says she enjoyed the teaching aspect and promoting safety of the sport.

Joey Cabell

Joey Cabell was raised in Hawaii and won a number of key surfing contests in the 1960s. He got involved with the Hobie Surf Team on a trip to promote surfing and skateboarding on the east coast. The tour was wildly popular and the team performed for thousands of people. Joey was one of the pioneers of slalom skateboarding and is credited with its popularity in the 1960s.

Mike Doyle

Mike started surfing in 1954 and became such a powerful force that he was nicknamed the "Ironman of Surfing."

In 1963 Mike joined up with Larry Stevenson of Makaha Skateboards to produce the first skateboard with hard rubber wheels. Larry believed that aligning himself with a top surfer would be a great way to promote his skateboard line. It looks like he was right — in the course of three years, four million dollars' worth of Makaha product was sold.

After a successful skate career, Mike helped with the design of the mono ski. The mono ski was a single, double-wide snow ski, which may be seen as a precursor of today's snowboards. In the late 60s, Hanson Surfboards produced a Mike Doyle signature model surfboard. It has since become one of the world's top collectable surfboards.

John Freis

John was the first international skateboard champion. He took first place in the class AA overall in the 12 year old and over division at the international championships in 1965. He is credited with inventing a number of tricks, including the nose wheelie.

John started with the Makaha Skateboard Team and then joined up with the Hobie Skateboard Team prior to the International Championships. After his win, John and the Hobie Skateboard Team performed skate demos for the Montgomery Ward stores across the United States. This led John to the east coast to demo his talents at the World's Fair in New York with fellow members of the Hobie Team.

Randy Lewis

A member of Jack's Skateboard Team, Randy is famous for his one cover shot on SkateBoarder magazine, along with the one that didn't make it. In 1964 Randy was featured with the Jack's team in the 1964 *SkateBoarder Magazine,* issue Vol. 1 #2.

A year later, plans were underway to put Randy on the cover again, this time skating in an empty swimming pool. Sadly, *SkateBoarder* Vol. 1 #5, was never published. This was clearly a result of the first crash of skateboarding. Besides being a famous skateboarder, Randy continued his fame by designing and shaping his own line of surfboards, which he is still producing today.

Mickey Maga

Mickey grew up in Huntington Beach, California. At the age of four he tap danced for the USO shows. He also was a child actor in the Hitchcock movie *The Birds* and did the voices of the dogs in the Disney animated classic, *101 Dalmatians.*

Mickey was a well-known skateboarder in Huntington Beach. He met up with Rick Woods, an older skateboarder who introduced Mickey to roller rink wheels that gripped the road a little better than the standard wheels he was using. Mickey modified his skateboard to match Rick's, and was on his way to fame.

Mickey was chosen by Jack's Surfboard to be a part of the new Jack's Skateboard Team. Other members of the team were Randy Lewis, Bobby Ross, and Jeff and Tim Knoble. In 1964, Mickey and the team were asked to do a demonstration for the spectators at the Huntington Beach U.S. Surfing Championships. They also demonstrated their skateboarding skills on the Dale Davis *Surf City* television show - a weekly surfing show.

Surf legend Duke Kahanamoku saw Mickey's demonstrations at the U.S. Surfing Championships and offered him a position on the new Duke Kahanamoku Skateboard Team. With Mickey on the team, Jim and Jeff Knoble moved over to Duke's team with another new member, Dennis Kletser. This team went on to compete in the 1965 International Skateboard Championships.

Peter Parkin

Back in the summer of 1947, Peter Parkin was having fun with his friend building scooters of different sizes and shapes. They built scooters that you could sit on, stand on and lay down on. But one of the most special scooters they built that summer was one that you could ride like a surf-board — it didn't have a handle. So it could be said that Peter Parkin was one of the world's first skateboarders.

During this time Peter could be seen riding his board around the La Jolla, California, Windandsea surf spot. As one of skateboarding's pioneers, he laid the foundation for the sport to blossom in the 1960s. Peter would later become one of the renowned "Windandsea Surf Club" members.

Linda Benson

Linda was a small blond-haired girl from southern California. A real-life Gidget, she surfed with a style like the professional male surfers. Linda placed well in a number of surf competitions in the late 1950s and 60s.

In 1964 Linda became part of history when Hansen Surfboards produced the first women's signature skateboard: the Linda Benson Model.

Bernard "Midget" Farrelly

Australian Bernard Farrelly was known as "Midget" to his friends because of his small size. He began surfing in 1956 on long hollow boards and at the age of 19 he was Australia's top surfer.

In 1965 Midget teamed up with *Surfing World* magazine to put on the Midget Farrelly Surfing World National Skateboard Championships. It was a 12-week competition and the winners of the state championship won a flight to Sydney to compete in the National Skateboard Championships.

Soon after, Midget brought out his own signature skateboard. The only other Australian skateboard lines in the 1960s were the Surfa-Sam and Cooley boards. Midget's board was equal to the high quality of the Makaha product line in the U.S.

Midget's championships and popularity eventually led him to join up with the Gordon and Smith Surfboard Company to produce the new Midget Farrelly Model.

Charles "Corky" Carroll III

Growing up in Surfside, California, Corky spent most of his free time in the morning and after school surfing. By the age of 11, Corky was being sponsored by Crowe Surfboards; eventually he got a sponsorship with Hobie Surfboards. Among Corky's many accomplishments was being a five-time U.S. overall surfing champion.

Corky was involved with Hobie Alter in developing and promoting his line of surf and skateboard products. He traveled with ground-breaking surfers Hobie, Joey Cabell and Mike Hynson on a cross-country trip. Before the gang headed south, Corky showcased his skateboarding skills on the Johnny Carson Show.

Some of Corky's most memorable moments come from skateboarding at night rallies with the Hobie Surf and Skateboard Team. This was done on Hidden Valley Road in Laguna Beach in 1965. The team used tin cans as cones and car headlights to illuminate the road. In the 1970s Corky reviewed records for *SkateBoarder* magazine.

John Richards

John "L. J." Richards, or "Little John" as he is known, is one of the most versatile surfers in the world. He has a smooth style in any size surf, from the California coast to Hawaii's North Shore.

In 1964 Hansen Skateboards made their first skateboard line and one of their boards was the L.J. Richards Model. L.J.'s was one of the first professional skateboard signature models to be produced.

In the early 1970s, a surfer by the name of Frank Nasworthy replaced his clay skate wheels with urethane ones. As a result of this action, Frank helped launch the second skateboard wave. Thanks to his genius, the ride became infinitely smoother and skaters were finally able to grip the road. Board and truck design began to flourish and by mid-decade, skateboarding was suddenly hot again.

At first, freestyle, slalom and downhill skating ruled the scene. Then vertical skating began to hit. Originally vert riding was limited to backyard swimming pools, then it quickly began to completely dominate through the introduction of skateparks. Cement skateparks were a dream come true for skaters.

SkateBoarder magazine, which had produced four issues in the 1960s, was resurrected and became the bible of the sport. The magazine profiled a number of skate legends, many of whom are featured in this book. The ollie was developed in the late 1970s and as the decade ended, street skating began to take root. In fact, there were so many new developments in such a short period of time that many call the 1970s skateboarding's golden age. Sadly, it was not to last.

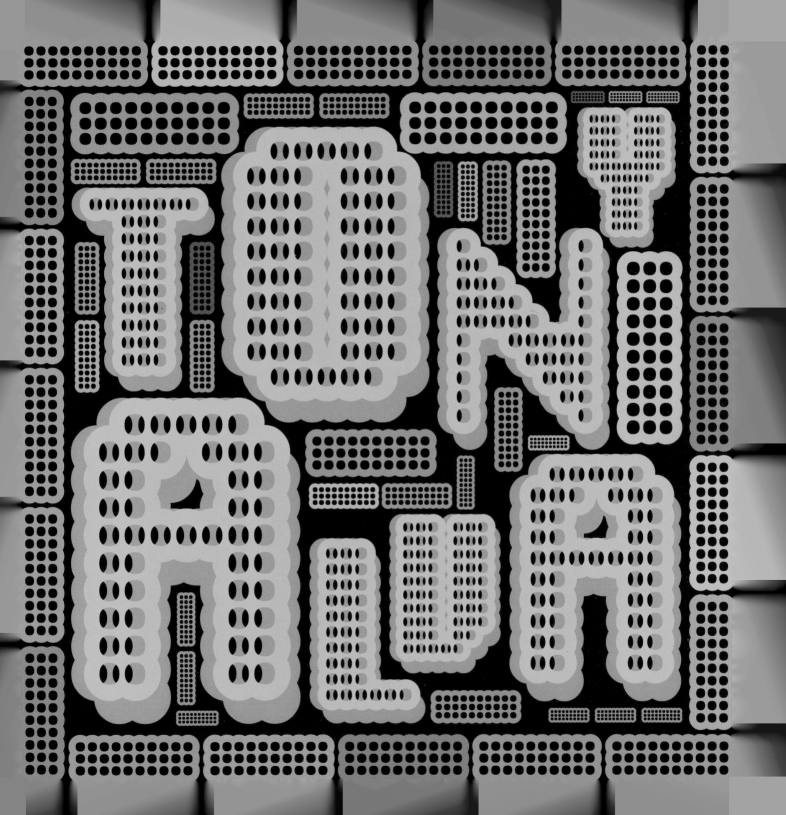

Tony "Mad Dog" Alva has had such a tremendous impact on skateboarding that it's impossible to put it all into two pages of this book. In fact, the story of Tony Alva in some ways reflects the story of skateboarding. Throughout Tony's ups and downs, he has remained 100 per cent core and he's never sold out. For many, he is the true soul of skateboarding.

Tony Alva grew up in Santa Monica, California. He lived near an amusement park called the Pacific Ocean Park. The park was renovated in 1958 but nine years later it had turned pretty grungy. There were surf breaks near the pier, but the area was completely different from Malibu or La Jolla. The locals called it Dogtown, alluding to its seedier aspects. Tony spent a lot of time surfing at the pier and hooked up with another local kid named Jay Adams.

At the age of 12, Tony and Jay heard the older POP surfers talking about a school in Brentwood called Paul Revere. The schoolyard had 15-foot asphalt banks, an exciting prospect for the young skaters. They started skating the banks like they surfed. This was the early 1970s and skating had pretty much died out everywhere else. It would be three years before the urethane wheel hit and changed everything. The Dogtown skaters were truly skate pioneers.

Tony and his friends hung around the Zephyr surf shop run by Jeff Ho, Craig Stecyk and Skip Engblom. Although the shop had a surf team of older surfers, a decision was made to create a younger team. This was an unusual move at the time. Eventually, this team evolved into the Zephyr Skate Team. Among its many stars were Tony, Jay Adams, Stacy Peralta and Shogo Kubo.

In 1975 the team entered the Bahne–Cadillac Skateboard Championships and proceeded to blow everyone away. Their looks,

aggressive skate style and hard core attitude were unlike anything else at the time. Almost overnight, Tony and the rest of the Zephyr team were hailed as superstars. *SkateBoarder* magazine began to feature the team and this fueled the flames even higher.

Besides being a vert pioneer,

Tony excelled in almost every other facet of skateboarding in the 1970s. He jumped over 19 barrels, which got him into the Guinness Book of World Records. Tony competed in freestyle, downhill, slalom and cross country. In 1976, he won the World Professional title. In 1977, *SkateBoarder* ran an interview with him that propelled his legendary status to even greater

heights. His nickname was "Mad Dog" and coupled with his intense, aggressive attitude, Tony changed the face of skateboarding.

In 1976, Tony left the Zephyr team and joined up with Logan Earth Ski/International Association of Skateboard Companies. Some didn't feel Tony was a positive influence on the sport. But this view was in the minority. Even with the breakup of the team, the Dogtown influence still raged and Tony was its key representative.

It wasn't a surprise that Hollywood came calling, trying to cash in on the success of skateboarding. Tony was featured in the film *Skateboard* as Tony Bluetile.

In 1977, Tony started up his

own skateboard company. Alva Skates was one of the first skater-owned and -operated companies, and it struck a chord with independent-minded skaters.

The advertising for the Alva boards was revolutionary. Many skaters can still recall the company's slogan: "No matter how big your ego, my boards will blow your mind."

In the early 80s, skateboarding experienced a huge bust. Although Tony and his partner Pete Zehnder had achieved great success, they had also squandered a lot of money on short-lived products. Tony ended the partnership and completely removed himself from skateboarding, moving back home with his father and taking dental technician courses at a junior college.

Thankfully, Tony returned to the skate world in the mid-80s and relaunched Alva Skates. He built a super-charged team.

Tony Alva's influence on skateboarding now spans over three decades. He still rides as many pools as he can. While so many other people have long given up on skateboarding, Tony Alva's passion continues to burn and this is what will make his skate legacy so great.

The fact is, Jay Adams' contribution to skateboarding defies description or category. Jay Adams is probably not the greatest skater of all time, but I can say without fear of being wrong that he is clearly the archetype of modern-day skateboarding. He's the real thing, an original seed, the original virus that infected all of us. He was beyond comparison.

—Stacy Peralta, writing in *Thrasher* magazine

An original Dogtowner, Jay Adams' exploits were well known in the 1970s. Jay was always controversial both on and off a skateboard.

Jay's skate roots lay in surfing. He spent a huge amount of time at the Pacific Ocean Park, where his stepfather, Kent Sherwood, ran a surf rental concession. At the age of eight, he was already an excellent surfer.

It was at POP, known locally as Dogtown, that Jay met up with Tony Alva. The two would protect the surfing spot together, ensuring that only locals could surf there. As Alva explained in a story in *Spin* magazine, "We'd sit up on the pier with these wrist rockets and this pile of polished stones, and just bombard anyone who was from outside our territory with whatever was available. Rocks, bottles, rotten fruit. Jay was a notoriously good shot."

In exchange for guarding the spot, Adams and Alva were allowed to surf there. Through hanging out with the older surfers, the two learned about magnificent asphalt banks of the Paul Revere Junior High School in Brentwood. Adams and Alva focused their attention on these banks and began riding them with an aggressive surf style. They soon discovered other schools like Kenter and Bellagio that had similar facilities.

Eventually, Adams and Alva were joined by other skaters. The group hung out at the Zephyr surf-shop, run by Jeff Ho. The shop was owned by Skip Engblom, who admitted to *Spin* magazine that it was a very different type of business. "Once we ended up buying a quarter of a barge of firecrackers. We didn't know how much that was exactly. But the price sounded really cheap."

The shop was very popular with the Dogtown skaters and they would work shaping and repairing boards in exchange for free stuff or discounts. Ho decided to sponsor two surf teams — a senior team and a junior team that comprised a number of skateboarders, including Adams, Alva, Stacy Peralta and Shogo Kubo. This junior surf team eventually became the Zephyr skate team.

Like his Dogtown peers, Jay skated with a much more radical style and intensity than had been seen before. His performances, along with those of fellow Dogtowners, at the 1975 Bahne-Cadillac contest were revolutionary. They were so different and aggressive that they confounded the judges and blew the audience away. In fact, it is this contest that was responsible for launching the legend of the Z-Boys and Dogtown.

By the time 1976 had rolled around, skateboarding had exploded worldwide. Jay's father, Kent Sherwood, went into business with Ho and Engblom to produce a line of Zephyr skateboards. Things did not run smoothly at all and eventually Sherwood left the company, took Jay with him and created Z-Flex. The Zephyr team never recovered and all the skaters went their separate ways.

Jay enjoyed a huge following and Z-Flex achieved a great deal of success. In the late 1970s, he came out with a pro signature helmet — The Flyaway. At the age of 18, Jay moved out to Hawaii. In the decades since, Jay has experienced many ups and downs. However, although he has stayed out of the spotlight, Jay Adams remains one of the greatest skaters ever to ride a board.

Stacy Peralta

Stacy Peralta grew up in Santa Monica (aka Dogtown) and surfed with people like Tony Alva and Jay Adams. The group would also skate local schools that featured enormous asphalt banks. It was here they developed their aggressive riding techniques. Hanging out with the gang, Stacy eventually found himself on the Zephyr surf team. Zephyr soon started to make skateboards and in 1975, Stacy placed third at the Del Mar contest. This contest put Dogtown on the map. Unfortunately, things turned sour at Zephyr and many of the team members moved on. Stacy moved on to Gordon and Smith and quickly found success with his Warptail I and II models.

Besides being featured in numerous skate magazines, Stacy starred in two skate movies: *Freewheelin'* and *Skateboard Madness.* He also toured extensively. However, it was his decision to leave Gordon and Smith in 1978 and join up with George Powell that attracted the most attention. Many people thought Stacy was crazy to leave G&S, especially when things were going so well for him. However, Stacy felt the move was crucial in his development. "You've always gotta move on and do something different," he told *SkateBoarder* magazine in 1979.

Stacy began developing a powerful team of riders at Powell Peralta, including people like Alan Gelfand, Mike McGill and freestylist Tim Scroggs. Towards the end of the 70s, skateboarding died and Powell Peralta struggled. The lean years were tough but it allowed Stacy to focus his efforts on creating the best company he could build.

Thanks to his amazing ability to discover talented skaters, Stacy was able to create one of the best skateboard teams ever assembled. This team included Tony Hawk, Lance Mountain and Rodney Mullen, along with dozens more pros and amateurs. There is no question that Stacy's nurturing of talent laid the foundation for a strong skate industry. He is probably the best team manager that the industry has ever had.

But Stacy's talents extended further. He worked with artist/photographer Craig Stecyk and created the first skateboard video, which further propelled the company and the sport. Powell Peralta's team, the Bones Brigade, traveled around the world and set off near riots every time they released a new video.

At the start of the 1990s, Stacy and George Powell began to have different ideas about the company's future. When they couldn't come to an agreement, Stacy decided to leave. At the time the skate industry was going through an enormous shakeup and there was a highly negative atmosphere.

Stacy began to devote his talents to film production. In 1999 however, *Spin* magazine featured an article on Dogtown. The interest spawned by the article was huge. A year later Stacy found himself working with Craig Stecyk and Agi Orsi on a documentary about Dogtown. With financial backing from Vans, the shoe company, the documentary has caused the same kind of magic that the old Powell Peralta videos used to create. The key difference is that now the outside world is taking note. At the 2001 Sundance Film Festival the film won awards for best documentary and Stacy picked up an award for best director. All skaters would agree that this is definitely a fitting tribute.

Bob Biniak

A key figure from Dogtown, Bob started skating in 1971. He was a very strong vertical skater who excelled in pipe riding but was also known as a formidable downhill speed racer. Bob rode for Logan Earth Ski. In an interview with *SkateBoarder* magazine in December 1977, Bob was asked, "Are there any radical things you'd like to do in the future?" His reply foretold of a life after skateboarding: "Yeah, I'd like to shoot a 63 at the Riviera Country Club." Bob has since gone on to become a professional golfer. Most recently his signature board from Dogtown sold on the eBay auction website for over $3,500.

Ellen Oneal

Ellen's interest in skateboarding began with some roller skate wheels hammered onto a 2x4. In 1975, Ellen entered a contest put on by the San Diego *Union Tribune* newspaper. Two hundred guys and Ellen entered. She competed against 80 guys in her division and took second place.

In 1977, Ellen was brought on to the Gordon & Smith team via top slalom pro Chris Yandall. Despite her image of being fairly conservative, Ellen says the truth was a little different. "I took risks and I got kicked out of hotels along with everyone else," she says with a note of defiance.

Ellen teamed up with Tony Alva and Leif Garrett to work on the film *Skateboard*. For those unfamiliar with this work of cinematic art, Ellen sums it up succinctly: "It was a trashy b-movie produced and directed by people who knew nothing about skateboarding."

In 1980, Ellen became the advertising director at *SkateBoarder* magazine. "Basically, they brought me in to calm advertisers down. They were upset with the lack of focus by the inclusion of things like BMX and rollerskating." In 1987 Ellen found work at a top-level executive placement service. Over the past 14 years, Ellen has progressed through the ranks and now works as a branch manager.

Brad, Brian, Bruce & Robin Logan

The Logans were known as skateboarding's First Family (even their mother skated). Their association with skating spanned two eras — the 1960s and 70s.

Bruce was perhaps the best-known Logan. At 12 he won his first skate contest in 1964 at the International Surf Festival. Bruce's speciality was freestyle and he was known as the master of the nose wheelie. The two other brothers, Brian and Brad, were also accomplished riders.

At the start of skateboarding's second boom, the family started up Logan Earth Ski. Their boards featured solid wood decks and were very popular.

Robin was involved in skateboarding at a young age. At seven, she would do demos in department stores with her brother Bruce and Ty Page. Robin followed her brother's path and excelled in freestyle, but she also competed in high jump, barrel jumping and slalom racing. It was reported in *SkateBoarder* that Robin was the first woman ever to do a kickflip.

Robin

Bruce

Steve & Micke **Alba**

Steve Alba exploded onto the skate scene in 1978. Before taking up skateboarding, Steve rode BMX bikes in pools, but according to his profile in *SkateBoarder,* "found them too limiting." It's a good job that Steve dropped BMX, since he went on to become one of the true kings of vert.

When Steve was twelve, he spotted a skater performing nose wheelies and this got him interested in skateboarding. One of the most interesting aspects of skateboarding during the 1970s was the geographic rivalries between areas. There was Dogtown (Santa Monica), Down South (San Diego), and Steve's area, "The Badlands."

In 1976, Steve began skating the Mount Baldy pipeline along with the L-Pool. At the time skateparks were not really offering challenging vertical terrain. Thanks to Steve's input with skatepark builder Stan Hoffman, the Pipeline Skatepark gave skaters a remarkable challenge: the world's first full pipe.

Steve's abilities grew dramatically and by 1978, he was consistently placing at the top of the rankings in the Hester Pro Bowl series.

Steve had two nicknames. One was "Le Machine" due to the fact that he had such endurance when he skated, often for hours at a time. The other nickname was "Salba," which came from his S. Alba signature model.

Steve has had a number of sponsors over the years, including Santa Cruz and Independent. In 1979, he performed in Devo's "Freedom of Choice" video. Steve hung out with fellow skaters Duane Peters and Steve Olson. This was an explosive combination of skate talent and they brought a "punk rock" attitude to skateboarding.

Steve still skates heavily and was most recently featured in the video "Fruit of the Vine," a homage to the joy of riding backyard pools. He has worked with the Warped Tour since its inception. No doubt as you are reading these words, Steve is probably draining a pool, waiting patiently to skate it.

Following on the heels of his brother Steve, Micke Alba hit the skate world with a bang. At the age of 12, he was featured in the "Who's Hot" section of SkateBoarder and sponsored by Kryptonics. Micke was fortunate enough to witness various skate sessions at backyard pools involving his brother and his friends. Micke progressed quickly as a skater and was featured on a number of SkateBoarder covers. During the early to mid-80s, Micke entered a few contests and started a promising career in the sport of long-distance roller skating. In 1985, Micke got back into skateboarding and was sponsored by Santa Cruz and later Dogtown.

Dave Andrecht

"The Raver," as he was known, got into skateboarding in 1976. He started skating streets and moved up to Carlsbad Skatepark and then the epic Spring Valley park. Thanks to slalom star Conrad Miyoshi, Dave managed to get onto the Sims team. For a time, his signature board became the number one seller for Sims. Dave also worked on the "Freedom of Choice" video by Devo (along with a variety of other skaters including Alva, Elguera, Olson and Peralta). He was known for his huge backside airs and his signature

Don "Waldo" Autry began his skateboard career on a Black Knight skateboard in the early 1970s. By 1975, his status as a vert legend was sealed at the Mount Baldy Pipeline. But Waldo's reputation went way beyond vertical riding. There are stories of an intoxicated Waldo doing a handstand three-quarters of the way up Signal Hill and how he counter threatened a member of the Cripps street gang and

Waldo Autry

walked away unhurt. The Pipeline had a diameter of about 14 feet, but Waldo soon found pipes that were 22 feet in diameter. Waldo was sponsored by Tunnel and rode for the Pepsi skateboard demo team. Although known as a vert skater, he did manage a few freestyle tricks at the demos. Waldo resurfaced in the skate world in the late 1990s. He took to the sport of downhill racing and posted some very impressive speeds.

Brad Bowman

Brad Bowman scrimped and saved for his first skateboard — a clay-wheeled Super Surfer. He soon joined up with a surf shop skate team that would provide him with free product. From here, things progressed to a sponsorship with Vans skate shoes. In 1977, he entered his first professional contest — the Catalina Classic. He wound up placing 25th in the downhill event, but soon after found himself riding for Gordon and Smith. In 1978, Brad began entering vert contests and placed well. He then moved over to Sims where he gained an immense following. Bowman's signature model was a best seller.

Steve Cathey

Throughout grade school, Steve Cathey rode a skateboard, but he used it mostly for transportation. At the age of 15, Steve started getting into skateboarding in a big way. At the beautifully paved hill of La Costa, he managed to capture the attention of photographer Warren Bolster, who snapped his shot and put it in *SkateBoarder* magazine. Soon after, he was entering skate contests and found himself sponsored by Gordon & Smith.

Steve was accomplished in both freestyle and vert skating. At G&S, Steve helped to promote the highly successful Yo Yo Wheels. Nowadays, Steve has a thriving career in the skateboard shoe industry.

Eddie Elguera

"El Gato," as he was known, was introduced to skating at the age of 10 with his two older brothers. The brothers received their Hobie skateboards by mailing in four dollars and four coupons from Buddy-Buddy Ice Cream. Eddie wound up riding for Hobie a few years later and then Variflex. His low-key style and quiet nature was in marked contrast to other vert skaters at the time, who were very much into punk mind-set. Eddie let his skating do the talking. He was best known for his handplant variations, including the layback aerial and 360 hand-plant from fakie.

Dave & Paul
Hackett

Paul

Paul Hackett was first featured in the August 1977 issue of *SkateBoarder*. It was a black and white shot of him jumping off a ramp in mid-air with his hands all the way up. Looking carefully at the shot, you can see that Paul's running shoes have black strips attached. These black strips were called Suspenders and they were part of a special grip system made from Velcro. The photo looked incredible and readers were astonished at Paul's airborne antics. By the next issue Paul had made the cover. In the era before the ollie, the Suspender product along with Skyhooks were the only way for skaters to truly get lift off and the brothers showcased the product for all it was worth.

Besides gaining a reputation with Suspenders product, David was an amazing competitor in both slalom and vert. In the 1970s, he won a number of competitions, including the Hang Ten World Championships and two Oasis Skatepark contests.

Both Paul and David were sponsored by Gordon & Smith. In the 80s Dave went on to a successful career with Skull Skates, as well as designing for clothing companies, including Jimmy Z. Sadly, Paul passed away in the spring of 2001 after a battle with cancer.

Dave

Henry Hester started skateboarding in the first skateboard era, on metal wheels nailed to 2x4s. He progressed to a Makaha Super Surfer. The film *Skater Dater* got him even more excited about skateboarding. Henry would practice slalom on the hill in front of his house, painting little 2" rings as cones.

When skateboarding hit again in the mid-1970s, Henry got right back into it. He would spend hours each Sunday racing with friends at La Costa. One of his main competitors was Bob Skoldberg, and eventually the two began dominating every slalom contest they entered. And, in what surely is a first, the two devised a plan to share the proceeds. The winner would get 75 per cent and the loser would get 25 per cent.

Nicknamed "The Bad H," Henry had a very successful career with Gordon and Smith Skateboards. His signature slalom board was very popular. Retailing for about $25 in 1976, the boards have since become highly collectible, hitting prices of well over $500.

Henry was also involved in the Signal Hill races and devised a skate car he called "White Lightning." This fiberglass contraption hit a speed of 57 mph. As slalom and downhill declined in popularity, Henry changed direction and found himself at the center of the vert world. He created the world's first vertical skate contest. He felt skateparks were the perfect venue for contests. With the help of the same people who ran the La Costa weekend events, he put together the first pool contest, in Spring Valley.

Strangely enough, the contest organizers didn't allow spectators at the first contest. It was designed to be a media event only — there was only a two-foot space to work in. The judges had scorekeepers with them and would just call out numbers from one to one hundred for every trick. Weeks later, in fact before the next Hester Series contest, Tony Alva and Henry worked out the judging system that's still used today.

Henry invented a few fun side events, like carving for distance, how many one wheelers you could do in a minute, and doubles. "Inventing doubles was one of the best things I ever did for skateboarding," he says. The vert contests that Henry created were eventually sold to Frank Hawk (Tony's father), who renamed them the Gold Series. This series became the contest circuit for the National Skateboard Association.

By 1978, Henry began to move away from the skate industry and found work in the computer field. Then, in 1985, Larry Gordon hired him to run G&S Skateboards. Henry turned things around at the company but eventually left, turning his attention to the snowboarding industry.

Henry Hester

Skitch Hitchcock

Skitch was best known for his wild "gorilla grip" move. He would skate in bare feet and grip the ends of his board with his toes and jump off ramps, achieving considerable air. He was also known for designing unusual ramps and high-speed skate cars. Skitch also designed uniquely shaped boards and a line of trucks.

Although he started at the age of six, Skitch didn't get serious about skateboarding until he was twelve. His gymnastics background helped him pull some very difficult moves on a skateboard, including v-sits and a handstand using two 10" skateboards.

Skitch was involved with the Skateboardmania tour that featured the infamous loop. While most skaters weren't able to do the loop, Skitch (along with Duane Peters) accepted the challenge of the loop and conquered it.

Hobie sponsored Skitch throughout his professional career, which culminated in a highly successful European tour.

Russ Howell had a number of claims to fame in his skateboard career. He was one of the first truly professional skaters — actually making a living off the sport with tours and sponsors. He appeared on the *Tonight Show with Johnny Carson* and the game show *To Tell the Truth*. Russ started skateboarding in 1959, and once the urethane wheel hit in the early 1970s, he devoted a huge amount of time to freestyle. Besides performing a wide range of gymnastics moves, Russ was best known for spinning 360s. He traveled to many places to promote skateboarding, including a major tour of Australia.

Russ got out of skateboarding in the late 1970s, mainly because he didn't like the hardcore punk attitude and rebelliousness. He also ran into some pretty unethical business people — including one company that embezzled six million dollars from him. Russ left California for Idaho but remained with the sport in his own special way. How many people in their 50s do you know who have a half pipe in their backyard?

Russ Howell

Duane Peters

Duane Peters was and remains a committed hard-core skater. His exploits are storied and his views about skateboarding have been quite controversial. In 1998, Duane was interviewed by *Big Brother* and asked about his past: "I never hung out with the Bones Brigade. I was at war with the Bones Brigade. When I was competing, it was Santa Cruz and Independent against the world back then. We didn't care about nobody."

Nicknamed "The Master of Disaster," Duane began skating on a Black Knight skateboard at the age of six. During skateboarding's second wave he quickly developed a taste for vert. He was one of the stars in the Skateboardmania show and was the first skater to make a 360-degree loop in the show. Duane accomplished the loop with and without the safety track. Although Duane was able to conquer the loop, he did wind up breaking his collarbone riding it. In fact, Duane has broken his collarbone at least nine times.

He is the innovator of the Indy Air and continually pushed the limits of vert skating. Besides leaving a huge mark in skateboarding Duane has achieved a fair amount of success with his group the US Bombs. He remains a hard-core, aggressive skater to this day and consequently enjoys the respect of thousands of skaters worldwide.

Ty Page

Ty Page was known as "Mr. Incredible" and the nickname suited him perfectly. He was a brilliant freestyle skater with lightning-fast footwork. The rumor about Ty was that he had learned a great deal of tricks from Bruce Logan in the early 1970s. Ty was a very quick study and by the time urethane wheels hit in the mid-70s, he was at the top. Although his first major sponsor was Unity Skateboards, he was best known for his signature board from Free Former along with Black Gold wheels.

Ty developed a number of key tricks, including "The Ty Slide" and an early shove-it move called the "Ty Hop." He was a master of the pirouette, kick flip and nose wheelies on banks.

Ray "Bones" Rodriguez

Ray Rodriguez started skating with many other skate legends back in the mid-1970s. He skated places like the Fruit Bowl along with people like Alva and Adams. Although Ray's first sponsor was Powerflex, he is best known for being one of the first skaters sponsored by Powell Corporation. George Powell, the owner of Powell Skateboards, arrived at Ray's local skatepark with a briefcase filled with his new white wheels. Ray started riding for George right away, picking up the nickname "Bones" along the way. The wheels were also called Bones and they were bestsellers. Many skaters can vividly recall Ray featured in print ads riding parks on the "Quicktail" model.

When Stacy Peralta joined George Powell, Ray became one of the key members of the Bones Brigade. His signature board featuring a skull and sword was very popular and is now a highly collectible item. By the early 1980s, Ray had begun to suffer from lower back problems and he turned his attention to finishing school and music.

At the age of 13, Doug made it into the "Who's Hot" section of *SkateBoarder*. It was quite a remarkable entrance and the start of a brilliant skate career. Top freestyler Brian Logan was quoted as saying, "Doug is the hottest up and coming skateboarder of the moment."

At the age of eleven Doug was sponsored by the Bahne team and had a number of top skaters mentoring him, including Bob Mohr and Denis Shufeldt. After skating for Bahne, he wound up on the prestigious Gordon and Smith team.

Doug "Pineapple" Saladino was one of the very few freestyle skaters who made a successful transition to vertical skating.

Doug Saladino

Tom Sims

Tom Sims' contribution to board sports continues to have an impact to this day. A native of New Jersey, Tom migrated to the west coast. It was here that he began to experiment with skateboards. Tom was passionate about creating a different type of ride. He used whatever material he could find (including water skis) to develop a new type of board: the longboard. Over time, he became a committed longboarder and would enter freestyle contests

Tom's skate company was very successful. Many skaters from the 70s either owned one of his boards or a set of Sims Snakes. In the early 80s, Tom left the skate world to help develop an new sport — snowboarding.

bob skoldberg

Bob was a world champion slalom skater who had a phenomenal career with Hobie. He traveled extensively with the team and gave numerous safety demonstrations to tens of thousands of people. The Hobie tour of Europe was very successful and helped to develop skateboarding in that part of the world. He also designed the Hobie Flex Slalom board. In 1977, Bob competed in the Akron World Championships where he took first place. These Championships were televised on *CBS Sports*. Bob was also an extremely fast downhill racer. He competed in standup along with the specialized skatecar division.

Chris Strople

Sometimes it really pays to make friends with the skate patrol at your local skatepark. Chris Strople had the good fortune to meet up with vert ace Tom "Wally" Inouye at Montabello skatepark. Chris spent a lot of time watching Wally, and the two eventually started skating together. From here, Chris rose quickly through the skate ranks and got sponsored by Sims. He has been credited with helping to develop the tail tap, an early vert move. As time progressed, Chris and Wally teamed up with Caster Skateboards and released their own signature models.

Steve Olson

It's been almost a quarter century since Steve "Bulky" Olson became part of the skate world and his impact is still being felt today. Combining style with an intense attitude, Steve shook the very foundations of the late 70s skate world to its core. He was one of the pioneers who fused skateboarding with a "punk rock" attitude and managed to upset as many people as he impressed.

Steve's history with skateboarding began when he was five. He rode a metal-wheeled skateboard in San Francisco. By the mid-1970s he had settled in Southern California and moved his attention from surfing to skateboarding. He began riding the banks at the Huntington Pier. Thanks to his older brother and a few other friends, he started to tackle challenging terrains and began skating pools as well. His surfing background was evident in his riding — he had an extremely smooth and fluid style.

By the time he reached 16, Steve was the overall winner of the Hester Pro Bowl series — the top vertical skating circuit. Six months later *SkateBoarder* readers voted him skater of the year for 1978. His signature board on Santa Cruz was immensely popular — it featured a full edge-to-edge checkerboard design, an engineering feat at the time.

Steve worked in video and was recently featured stylishly riding a longboard in a TV commercial for a website. If you look closely, you'll catch Steve in other ads (including one with Ringo Starr).

Vicki Vickers

A native of Texas, Vicki got into skateboarding at the age of 14. She credits Dogtown legend Nathan Pratt for encouraging her. Vicki rose quickly up the vertical skate ranks. At the Newark contest, she collided in a doubles routine with Lani Kiyabu and they both wound up in the hospital for nine days!

In an interview with *SkateBoarder,* Vicki lamented the poor coverage of female skaters and the lack of respect that pro women skaters were receiving "I'll be damned if we're not out there breakin' our necks just like the guys…we're gettin' burned. How many issues has it been since you've seen a girl's face? About five."

Vicki was sponsored by Kryptonics and was also a featured rider in the SkateboardMania show.

MIKE WEED

Mike was one of a very few pros who excelled in both freestyle and vert skating. He had a great career with Hobie and toured around the world with the team. He eventually went on to start his own wheel company. His ad featured the infamous slogan, "My Weed's legal."

Alan Gelfand

Today's generation of skaters owes much gratitude to Alan Gelfand. It was his development of the "no hands air" or ollie pop in the late 1970s that changed skateboarding forever.

Alan was born in 1963 in New York. He moved to Florida at the age of five. In 1974, Alan started skateboarding. He was lucky to live in a state that built a number of skateparks. There was a park in Hollywood that in Alan's words was "built so crappy that a lot of the stuff was over vertical and uneven." There was a run that featured a pool and it was here that Alan started working on his soon-to-be-famous move. As he rode over the vertical ledge, the board would pitch back and Alan would bend his knees. The board would then spring back and he'd lift a few inches off the pool wall and turn 180 degrees. The move was lightning quick and revolutionary.

In the summer of 1977, skate superstars Stacy Peralta, Gregg Weaver and Wally Inouye were on a tour of east coast skateparks arranged by Warren Bolster of *SkateBoarder* magazine. At a skatepark in Fort Lauderdale, Stacy saw Alan perform the move. Alan's nickname was "Ollie" and that's where the trick got its name.

Thanks to Stacy Peralta, Alan was one of the first people called to be on Powell Peralta's new skate team, the Bones Brigade. Stacy had Alan fly out to California and skate Winchester skatepark. Alan went back to Florida and practiced ollieing off a ramp. Soon after, *SkateBoarder* magazine published photos of his amazing trick.

The entire skateboard world was astounded. Many people couldn't believe that Alan was able to achieve a no-hands aerial without the use of some type of attachment. In a 1998 interview with George Powell, Alan recalls people stealing his shoes, looking for Velcro strips or suction cups. Such was the mystery of the ollie! Eventually, skaters did figure out how Alan was doing the ollie, but it took some time.

Alan became a successful pro, but stopped skating in 1981. He admits his timing might have been bad but his knees hurt and he began to get interested in another four-wheeled contraption — the automobile. In 1986 he got into car racing and eventually became a top national competitor. His love of cars led him to his present work — selling and servicing Volkswagens.

Eric Dressen

There are very few skaters who can claim their skate career spans from their pre teen years and into their young adult lives. Eric Dressen is one such skater. He started skating at age seven and entered his first contest at the age of eight. Encouraged by his father, Eric quickly got into the sport. Over time, he joined up with some older skaters and began skating pools and pipes. Like most skaters in the 1970s, Eric would pore over every detail in *SkateBoarder* magazine, trying to figure out how to accomplish the moves found in the magazine. Never in his wildest dreams could he imagine actually being in the magazine. However, that's exactly what happened. Incredibly, at the age of 10, Eric was profiled in *SkateBoarder*'s "Who's Hot" section.

Eric's first sponsor was Logan Earth Ski and towards the end of the 70s, he moved to Alva. Sadly, the industry hit a slump and Alva went out of business. In 1980 Eric stopped skating and didn't return to the sport until the mid-1980s. During this hiatus, he sold all his back issues of *Skate-Boarder* and took up bicycle racing. But once Eric skated a backyard pool, he was hooked again on the fun of the sport. He rejoined his old sponsor Alva, started skating Upland skatepark and hung out with his old friends. By 1988, he was a top-rated street skater.

Eric is known as one as the pioneers of wall riding, which became one of the classic moves of the 80s. He started entering street contests and placed well. He eventually turned pro, riding for a number of key companies, including Alva, Dogtown and Santa Cruz.

Shogo Kubo

When Skip Engblom put together the legendary Z-Flex team, he chose Shogo Kubo and cast the skater in role of a "Zen-like being." Born in Kagoshima City, Japan, in 1959, Shogo arrived in the USA without the ability to speak English. He soon learned and picked up on the rhythm of life in southern California. While at his judo dojo, Shogo noticed that one of his fellow students was riding a skateboard to and from class. He was intrigued enough to try and soon found himself skating with Jay Adams.

After leaving Z-Flex, Shogo eventually wound up riding for Dogtown Skateboards. His board was a best-seller and his smooth, fluid style gained him a tremendous following. Towards the end of the 70s, Shogo wound up at the Cherry Hill skateboard park in New Jersey, where he became the resident pro.

In the 1980s Shogo moved to Hawaii and got out of skateboarding. However, he has recently joined up with Wes Humpton (formerly of Dogtown Skates). Over two decades have passed since he last skated as a pro, but Shogo now has a signature model with Bulldog Designs.

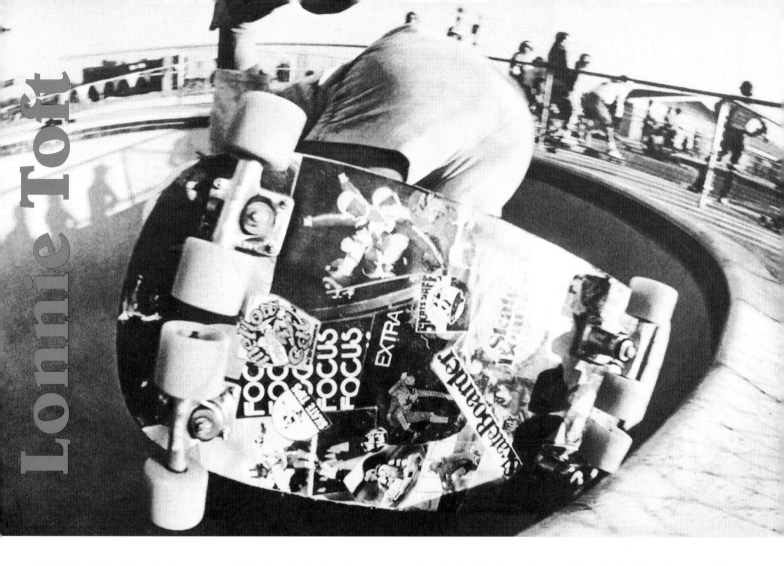

Lonnie Toft

Ride whatever you like; just get out there and have fun.
— SkateBoarder, August 1977

Lonnie Toft began his skateboarding career in the early 1960s. In 1974, Tom Sims asked him to join his skate team. Lonnie was an impressive freestyle skater and the originator of the G-turn. He was also an accomplished vert rider.

In 1976, Lonnie designed a skateboard that had a wider and fuller shape compared to most boards on the market at the time. On a trip to Toronto in that year, he had skateboard manufacturer Willi Winkels create a "Toft Design" board. When he came back to California and won a contest on the board, people were scrambling to get the new deck. Sims went full steam into production and

soon after, the traditional needle-nose skateboards were history.

There are two things that Lonnie is best remembered for. One was his "Outrageous" eight-wheeled skateboard. It was twenty inches in diameter and had shag carpeting on top. He'd ride it mostly on mellower terrain, but occasionally could be seen tearing up pools with it.

The other legacy that Lonnie

Toft left skateboarding was his promotion of snowboarding to the readers of *SkateBoarder*. In an interview with the magazine in 1979 he was asked about the sport (at the time called skiboarding). Lonny mentioned Dimitrije Milovich and the fact that he had produced only 150 boards to date "It's going to be a whole new sport as soon as it takes off, as soon as it gets accepted."

Laura Thornhill

Although Laura started skating in her native state of Texas, it wasn't until she moved to California with her family that she achieved fame. Laura was one of the top woman freestyle and slalom skaters and she won a large number of contests in the mid-70s. As a result of this, Laura became one of the first female skaters to have her own signature model: in 1977, Logan Earth Ski introduced the Laura Thornhill Model.

The Carrasco Brothers Rene, Richy & David

Rene

Known collectively as the Flying Carrasco Brothers, the Carrascos' passion for skateboarding still runs deep to this day. In the 1970s, the brothers performed over 2,000 demos as members of the Pepsi skateboard team. They were also pioneers of the homemade backyard skatepark. Their entire backyard was covered in wooden ramps.

While each brother excelled in pools, slalom, downhill and freestyle, they did have their specialities. Richy was known as a world-class 360 spinner and he was one of the first skaters to have his own signature wheel. Produced by Hobie, the Carrasco Spinners were specially designed wheels for spinning 360s. Since 1978, Richy has been the undefeated world champion of 360s. Despite the passage of time, Richy can still spin well over 150 revolutions without stopping.

Rene pioneered the use of Sky Hooks, which were special attachments that enabled him to achieve massive airs before the ollie. The brothers would do helicopters in mid-air and took the Sky Hooks in to empty swimming pools.

David was both a Californian state slalom and downhill racing champion.

Richy

George Orton

George Orton was born in Long Beach, California, and got his first taste of skateboarding in 1964 at the age of four. George loved riding his red Roller-Derby steel-wheeled skateboard but moved on to other sports. In 1972 George picked up a skateboard again so he could improve his surfing skills. It wasn't long before he started taking his parents' car and parking it out in the middle of the road. Here, he would jump the car with his skateboard!

George started skating around town, and his skills improved immensely. He wound up practicing relentlessly in local neighborhood pools. Since there were no skateparks in 1974, and missing the element of competition, George and his friends would ride the pools, seeing how high they could get.

George had developed a frontside style where he would grab the middle of his board when he reached the coping of the pool. The board and George started disconnecting from the lip of the pool, getting air between himself and the coping. This was the birth of the aerial. George decided to take his special trick to Skatopia skatepark when it opened. He was already well-balanced on vertical pool walls and George pulled off his aerial in the halfpipe, immediately sending a shock around the skateboarding world. The aerial changed skateboarding forever. In less than twenty-four hours, George was contacted by four different magazines wanting to come down to the skatepark to capture this phenomenon called "the Aerial."

Soon George moved on to Paramount skatepark where the largest vertical bowl in the world was built. The bowl was sixteen feet deep, with six feet of pure vertical. Most skaters couldn't even get half-way up. A week and a half after the park was opened, George was doing three-foot aerials out of the top of the bowl.

Tom Sims came down from Santa Barbara to see George perform his moves and quickly signed George to his team. George created the concept of two skaters riding at the same time during a routine (doubles). Crowds went wild when he skated together with Frank Blood.

From 1977 to 1980, George won a number of major contests and was recognized by all as truly an aerial madman. After skateboarding, George went on to excel at other sports such as tournament water-skiing and bull riding. In 1996 George returned to the skateboard world, competing in downhill events such as street luge and speed-boarding. George has gone on to compete in the X-Games, Gravity Games and Red Bull races, reaching the finals in each of them. But George still loves skating pools and blasting airs on his 44" longboard.

Tom "Wally" Inouye

Tom started skateboarding in 1972 on clay wheels. He was nick-named "Wally" by his grade eight friends because he was the only person who could kickturn on a concrete wall with one foot of transition. Wally was impressed enough with the skate footage in the movie *Super Session* to head down to Dogtown and skate the school banks of Paul Revere, Belagio and Kenter. In 1975, he met up with a well-known freestyler by the name of Dale "Sausage Man" Smith, who started to teach him tricks. Wally entered a number of freestyle and slalom contests and eventually made the move to more challenging terrain like pools and pipes. At the Long Beach Pool he met up with vert madman Waldo Autry and Wally learned some amazing moves from him.

In a 1977 interview with *SkateBoarder,* Wally was asked if bank, bowl and pool riding was getting the treatment it deserved from the various (skate) organizations. His response foreshadowed what was to come:

"[T]hey are still stuck on the flatland and slalom. Skating today is about pools, pipes and parks." He added, "I think some of those organization people are bad rapping us because they are afraid the bowlriders are going to take over the sport, and that the freestylers and slalomers will be left out."

Wally was well known for his incredibly smooth style. He created a very successful line of boards and t-shirts with the tag, "Wally's Pool Cleaning Service."

Bobby Piercy

Bobby was one of the best slalom skaters to emerge from the 1970s. His technique was very much like a parallel skier. You can get a good glimpse of his abilities in the film *Freewheelin'*. Tragically, Bobby died in a boating accident in the mid-1980s.

Gale Webb

In 1978, Gale Webb decided to take up skateboarding to prove to people that it wasn't a dangerous sport. She started riding the Concrete Wave Skatepark and the kids who skated there began teaching her tricks.

Gale picked up a sponsorship from Powerflex and eventually became team manager. Later, she had her own traveling skateboard show called "Skateboard Family." She had a portable halfpipe in the shows. A number of skate legends, including Neil Blender and Bert LaMar, rode the ramp in the early 80s. Up and coming skate stars like Tony Hawk and Christian Hosoi also rode for Gale's show.

In the mid-1980s, Gale hooked up with Vision and performed hundreds of shows in schools, malls and coliseums throughout the US. Through her tremendous dedication to the sport, Gale has earned the title of "the Skateboard Mama."

Denis Shufeldt

Denis Shufeldt combined speed skating with yoga techniques. Odd as it may seem, it paid off for Denis. He had an extremely fluid style and he won a number of races at places like La Costa.

In the mid-1970s, Denis's fairing technique was revolutionary. He developed a parallel stance with his knees bent and his hands behind his back. With this fairing stance, Denis would achieve speeds of over 50 mph (usually without safety gear!).

Robert Valdez

Bobby Valdez stared riding at the age of 12 and quickly progressed in both freestyle and vert skating. At the age of 14 he caught the attention of Dave Catterall of Powerflex, who began flowing him top-notch equipment. His skating got even better. At the 1978 Hester Series in Newark, New Jersey, Bobby switched his Tracker Trucks for a set of newly forged Independents. He did a frontside roll in and the first-ever invert. Bobby won the contest, Indy went on to gain a 50 per cent market share and the invert sealed Bobby's legendary status.

Dale "Sausage Man" Smith

Dale rode for Hobie and was a very popular figure with *SkateBoarder* magazine. At various times you could catch Dale in an article on freestyle or dressed up as Santa Claus or a Conehead (advertising the latest skate products). Dale was a key mentor for a number of skaters and a great promoter of skating worldwide. He is an avid collector of skate memorabilia and his collection of boards, magazines and other skateboard materials is well known.

Gregg Weaver

Known as the "Cadillac Kid," Greg Weaver was key in the resurgence of skateboarding during the early 1970s. His classic California blond, wavy hair and surf style scored him the first cover of the re-born *SkateBoarder* magazine in 1974. Gregg had a very successful career with Hobie and was also featured in the classic skate film *Downhill Motion*.

John Hutson

John Hutson started out racing on skateboards in the early 1960s in Northern California. After finishing high school, he moved closer to Santa Cruz and eventually started riding on urethane wheels. John started to get heavily into slalom racing and he would put slalom cones in lots of different places, like the banked walls of the Los Gatos Reservoir. John's best racing year was 1977, when he won 11 out of 14 races, including the spectacular Catalina Classic. On June 11, 1978, John stunned the skate world by achieving 53.45 miles per hour at Signal Hill standing on a skateboard.

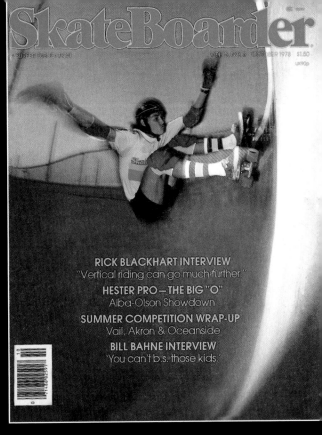

Rick Blackhart

How good was Rick Blackhart? Well, after only two and a half years of skateboarding, he was the subject of a nine-page interview in *SkateBoarder* magazine. Hailing from northern California, Rick Blackhart took to vertical riding very quickly. He reckons it took him about a month to learn the basics of vert. Rick used to have the nickname "Rubberman" due to his limber body, but thanks to a monthly advice column in *Thrasher,* more people know him as Dr. Rick.

Liability issues with skateparks, and the BMX and roller skating invasions led unfortunately to skateboarding's second major recession. People lost interest and the entire scene moved underground. A punk attitude fused with skateboarding and a spirit of "do it yourself" took over. As skateboarding went underground, it spawned a new generation of deeply committed skaters. Backyard ramps created a whole new crop of vert legends. With the bulldozing of so many skateparks, skaters also took to the streets.

By mid-decade, the advent of video had helped to bring about skateboarding's third wave. Kids could see new tricks on TVs set up in skate shops. Freestyle skating became extremely technical and helped lay the foundation for the next generation of skate moves. And of course, much of today's skate industry is headed up by former freestylers!

The mid- to late 1980s were an explosive time in the skate world: massive contests, huge sponsorship deals, enormous manufacturing facilities and magazines filled with ads. It was a pretty crazy time for skater and fan alike. As the decade rolled over, street skating began its ascent to major prominence. The skate world was due for a huge shake-up!

I would like to see [skateboarding] known to the public as what it really is, not just a hairstyle or some sort of clothes. I would like them to see the real difficult maneuvers, and try to understand and comprehend the physical strength and everything involved. I would like people to know what it's all about, not that it's just something we do to be rebellious.

—Tony Hawk in Transworld, 1989.

TONY HAWK

The most well-known skateboarder in the world was born May 12, 1968. His parents were both in their 40s and already had two children, each of whom was in their teens. As he writes in his autobiography, *Hawk*, "I was an accident." Tony was quite a handful as a youngster and even managed to get kicked out of pre-school for being so hyper.

In 1977, Tony's brother Steve introduced him to skateboarding. "My earliest skate memories are skating from alley to alley with my neighborhood friends to see which ones had quarter pipes in them. We would find at least three or four raging sessions within two blocks of my house, and the vibe was usually welcoming."

Luckily for Tony, he lived very close to the Oasis Skatepark. With the strong support of his father, Frank, Tony spent an enormous amount of time skating at Oasis. Tony credits Eddie Elguera for introducing him to vert skating. The first tricks he learned were rock n' rolls and airs.

Tony's first skate sponsor was Dogtown skateboards. This was late in the 70s, and the big skate bust had hit. However, the Dogtown team included not only Tony but Mark Rogowski, Christian Hosoi and Mike Smith. Tony briefly was sponsored by Independent Trucks but eventually struck an agreement with Tracker Trucks.

At the end of 1980, Tony received a call from Stacy Peralta, who informed him that Dogtown had gone out of business. Tony was being courted by Gordon and Smith Skateboards for possible sponsorship, but in the end, he decided to join up with the Powell Peralta team.

Besides being quite small for his age, Tony was pretty skinny. Although he was a very proficient skater, he was still finding his way through the ranks. One particular event that gives insight into the world of the early 80s skate scene was the time Tony was skating with Steve Alba and Duane Peters. Tony was not pro at the time and yet here he was with these two skate gods. For some reason Tony began laughing at them. Peters then spat at Tony, calling out, "This is punk rock, kid."

Tony took advanced classes in school, but during the early 1980s found himself absent as a result of tours and contests. As the decade progressed, skateboarding became more popular. Tony's father got more involved with the sport and started the National Skateboard Association. Thanks to the Powell Peralta videos "Bones Brigade Video Show" and "Future Primitive," Tony's popularity began to explode. His board royalties at Powell Peralta, which had started at less than a buck, went through the roof.

In an interview with *Transworld* in 1989, Tony explained that the inspiration for many of his tricks came in the middle of the night, as he fell asleep. He also picked up ideas by watching skate videos backwards.

In 1987 Tony began working on his most difficult trick — the 900. This was also the year of the "Animal Chin" video, which was a breakthrough video that further propelled Tony and the rest of the Bones Brigade to heights of popularity.

Tony was involved in three Hollywood films: *Thrashin'*, *Police Academy 4* and *Gleaming the Cube*. Although he admits to being a "terrible actor," Tony has good memories of working on the films.

Thanks to board royalties and contest winnings during the 1980s, Tony was able to concentrate his energy on skateboarding and not worry about holding a job outside of the industry. He even managed to purchase a house in Fallbrook (near Carlsbad, California) and with the help of friends, built an incredible backyard ramp there.

But during the early 90s, vertical skating diminished in popularity and Tony suffered a few setbacks. At one point, Tony's financial situation was extremely dark. Among other things, he was actually losing money when he performed demos. However, he kept skating and teamed up with Per Welinder to start Birdhouse Projects. With fierce determination, Tony kept going and he weathered the drought. Birdhouse built a strong team and the company is now one of the biggest in the skate world. In 1998, they released "The End" and it quickly became one of the most popular and biggest-selling skate videos of all time. Tony was featured completing a full loop on a specially designed ramp.

Starting in 1995 Tony began to receive an enormous amount of publicity outside the traditional skate media with the introduction of ESPN's Extreme Games. He won first place in the vert and millions of people (who before knew very little about skateboarding) began to appreciate his talents. In 1999, Tony performed the most astonishing trick of his career: He pulled off a 900 (two and a half times' rotation) at the X-Games. After six years of trying, Tony said that landing this trick was the most memo-

rable event of his career.

The power of television amplified this achievement and Tony became a bona fide celebrity. He was profiled by many non-traditional skate media, including *The New Yorker, Playboy* and CNN. His fame sky-rocketed with the introduction of the video game, "Tony Hawk's Pro Skater." It has become an enormously popular title and is part of the reason why so many younger kids are charging into skateboarding these days.

More recently, Tony has written a best-selling autobiography, launched his own clothing company and signed a color commentary agreement with ESPN. Although he has retired from the contest circuit, Tony remains a key figure in the skate world. He has given so much to skateboarding in his lifetime.

Despite his enormous popularity, Tony is a very down-to-earth person and he remains true to skateboarding. In the interview for this book, Tony's final comments say it all:

"I am not a video game, *I am a* human being."

At the age of 15, Christian Hosoi got sponsored by Dogtown. His fellow teammates included a guy called Tony Hawk. Sadly, the sponsorship only lasted for about six weeks. Even worse, as Christian started to make a name for himself, skateboarding hit its second bust. In 1980, prize winnings at vert contests usually didn't exceed $200. But Christian stuck it out, knowing that skateboarding was in his blood. By the time the mid-80s rolled around, Christian was one of the two top vert pros (the other guy was Tony Hawk). He was known for his incredibly high airs, fluid style and outrageous rock star persona.

Christian was larger than life. He was one of the first skateboarders to have his own board company (Hosoi skates, featuring the Hammerhead deck design.) He had his own wheel company (Hosoi Rockets) and he earned thousands of dollars each month.

At every contest he entered or demo he performed, Christian was a showman, holding nothing back and causing spectators to gasp at the height of his airs, including his signature trick, the "Christ Air."

Sadly, Christian's life outside of skateboarding has not been easy. He lost a good deal of his prize and sponsorship money due to mismanagement. In early 2000, Christian was caught carrying drugs at an airport in Hawaii and is now serving jail time. Skaters the world over hope one day to see the return of Christian.

BEN SHROEDER

Ben Shroeder gained a huge reputation as a pioneering skater with incredibly fast feet. His miniramp skills were exceptional. He is credited with developing much of the technical side of skateboarding during the early 1990s. Nowadays he can be found competing in masters vert competitions and slalom contests.

Bill Danforth

"It doesn't matter what you're riding, as long as you're riding."

Born and raised in Michigan, Bill Danforth started to get into skateboarding seriously in 1972. This was the year his older brother returned from college and brought home a Bahne board with Cadillac trucks and wheels. He skated around his basement and found himself hooked. When his brother took the board away on a later trip, Bill went out immediately and got himself the same Bahne board.

Bill was fortunate to live near the Endless Summer skatepark. He became a member of the skatepark team and has fond memories of skating parks in the surrounding cities, including Surf and Turf, High Roller and Apple skateparks. He started to place well in contests and in 1981 got the attention of the Variflex team when they were on tour at the Endless Summer park. Soon after, he was sponsored by both Madrid and Tracker Trucks. In 1984, Bill moved out to California to work for Tracker Trucks as the team manager. He was also the first darkroom assistant at *Transworld Skateboarding* magazine. Although he returned to college for a few months, he realized that skateboarding was booming and he wanted to devote his energy to it alone. In 1985, after placing third at the Oceanside street contest, Bill decided to turn pro.

Bill was known primarily as a vert rider, but he was equally as strong skating street. "Being from the midwest, we rode everything. We encouraged people to skate with us." In 1986, Bill joined the Alva team. "It was like a brotherhood — there was no attitude between the members of the team, but as a team, we had a lot of attitude."

Bill is heavily involved in organizing beginner skateboarders in association with cities in the midwest. He really enjoys doing this. He also is co-owner of Stink Brand Skateboards.

Billy Ruff

Billy started to get known in the skate world just as the second bust of skateboarding hit. He kept at it during the lean times — the early 1980s — and ruled Del Mar park (before Tony Hawk decided to drop by). He rode for G&S and Airwalk. Billy had a very smooth style and placed consistently high in competitions.

Cara Beth Burnside

Burnside

"It's good for girls to see that girls can skate....girls can skateboard! It's not just a guys' sport!"
Poweredge 1989

Cara Beth Burnside was taking rollerskating lessons next to the Big O skatepark in the late 1970s. She kept watching the skaters at the park and eventually decided to get into skateboarding. Although she was teased by many of her fellow male skaters, she did not give up. As she told *Poweredge* magazine in 1988, "I knew this was the sport I wanted to pursue." Soon after, Cara Beth entered her first contest at the Big O and found herself with a sponsorship with Powerflex.

Not all males were negative towards Cara Beth. Thanks to the support and influence of Duane Peters, Cara Beth was able to push herself and accomplish great moves on vert. Duane even helped her get a sponsorship with Santa Cruz.

Over time, Cara Beth surpassed the other female skaters she rode with and found herself skating with men only. Sadly, most of her fellow female skaters left the sport and Cara eventually decided that there was nothing in the sport for women, which made her feel very uncomfortable.

For the next few years, Cara Beth left skateboarding but returned to the skate world in 1988 to work with Gail Webb's Safety in Sports shows. She was the first female skater to be sponsored by Vans and eventually had her own signature shoe. Her talents on ramps rivaled those of many male skaters and she was the only woman to pull Miller flips.

In the 1990s, Cara Beth started snowboarding and her skate experience propelled her through the ranks. She has won a number of competitions. However, Cara Beth has not forgotten her skate roots. She still skates heavily and is sponsored by longboard manufacturer Flexdex.

Many people consider Chris Miller one of the smoothest vert skaters ever to ride a board. Chris was lucky enough to live very close to one of the best skateparks in the country — Upland. He would spend countless hours practicing there. In 1983, Chris won his first amateur contest at Upland Chris was the first skater to do backside lipsides on vert. For most of the 80s Chris was sponsored by Gordon and Smith. However, he left G&S to join Schmitt Stix. His board featured an upturned nose and laid the foundation for the change in skateboard shapes.

Chris started up his own company called Planet Earth, which was bought by K2 a few years back. Besides his extremely down-to-earth personality, Chris is known for being an outstanding surfer.

CHRIS MILLER

Eddie Reategui

Eddie Reategui was born in Peru and moved to Long Beach, California, as young kid. His skate career started out at Powell where he was a top amateur. He eventually joined up with the Alva skate team where he became their top rider. Eddie was a superb pool and vert skater. He can be seen in the film *Thrashin'* along with a number of other skaters from the Alva team.

Frankie Hill made his debut in the Powell Peralta video, "Public Domain." It was an explosive performance. He was described in *SkateBoarder* as "resembling a flea jumping off a window sill…the undisputed stunt man of the early 90s." Frankie set the stage for the new revolution in street style and many of today's pros owe a great deal to his ground-breaking moves

Sadly, the huge ollies and balls out style caught up with Frankie in 1993. He tried to ollie 10 stairs and a wall and wound up falling on his knee. This accident effectively crippled his career. Unfortunately, Frankie hadn't saved any of the money that had flowed from being a top pro for Powell Peralta skateboards. Frankie didn't have the $10,000 required for the knee surgery. He didn't realize that he was not covered under Powell's insurance policy, so he filed a Worker's Compensation claim. Eventually, he received enough money to cover the operation and to put himself through dental school.

Frankie Hill

Jeff Kendall

Jeff Kendall grew up in Indianapolis and he started skateboarding with a board that many people began with: the highly popular Cal 240. He progressed to a Ty Page Freeformer board and started riding ramps. In 1984 Jeff's uncle allowed him to build a ramp on his land. It was called the Love Ramp and was 28 feet wide. Jeff competed in a number of backyard contests in the mid part of the 1980s. At the time skateboarding was pretty dead and the Mid Eastern Skate Series (MESS) kept the sport alive.

Jeff became quite an accomplished skater and got sponsored by Madrid for a few years. He even picked up a sponsorship with Powell Peralta. Jeff was determined to get to California and was asked by Santa Cruz to fly out there. The timing was perfect - after he finished high school, he moved out to San Jose. Jeff dabbled in street skating, but his primary love was vert. He was able to find a solution to the lack of ramps by teaming with a bunch of friends and sharing the cost of rent of a warehouse.

Besides skating, Jeff was an accomplished musician. He joined up with Steve Cabellero to reform the Faction. When Jeff's pro career ended, he was able to stay with Santa Cruz and now works in their marketing department.

Jeff Grosso

Jeff Grosso got into skateboarding via the son of his mother's boyfriend. He was about two years older than Jeff and the two went to a skatepark. After this experience, Jeff was hooked. In grade five Jeff's family moved from Las Vegas to Arcadia, California. On the first day of school he met up with Eric Nash and asked him how he'd broken his wrist. "Skateboarding," replied Eric and this solidified their friendship. The two started riding backyard ramps and traveling out to Skatopia skatepark on the weekends.

As an amateur skater, Jeff got a lot of attention. He skated fast and won a number of contests. Jeff made his mark at the Terror in Tahoe Contest. He was known for his sad plants. As he progressed, he wound up with a number of sponsors, including Independent, Variflex and Santa Cruz. Jeff left Santa Cruz for Powell but he soon regretted the move and rejoined Santa Cruz. He currently rides for Black Label.

jeff PHILLIPS

Jeff Phillips helped to put Texas on the skate map and showed the skate world that not every great skater has to be from California. In 1973, Jeff received a skateboard from his grandmother for his tenth birthday. It was a steel-wheel board called the Shark. A few years later, Jeff got on the Wizard skatepark team and began heavy skate sessions at a place called the Rathole. It was here that the indomitable Texas skate attitude started to ferment. Jeff skated hard with fellow Texans Craig Johnson and John Gibson. Jeff landed a sponsorship deal with G&S, but things didn't work out too well, so he joined up with Sims. He encountered difficulties at Sims and eventually he left for Life's a Beach. Jeff was a masterful vert skater. He is best remembered for his signature "Phillips 66" move. Jeff was an immensely popular skater and is the only person ever to get the front and back cover of *Thrasher* magazine two times.

Jeff went into business for himself, starting up his own indoor skatepark in Texas. Locals recall it was a great place to ride and hang out. Sadly, on Christmas Day, 1993, Jeff took his own life. There is no question that skateboarding lost a tremendous figure that day. As Bill Danforth states, "Jeff was irreplaceable."

John Lucero

It's hard to believe that John Lucero's expulsion from a
skatepark led to a revolution in skateboarding, but it's
absolutely true. John began skating in the mid-1970s
and had an opportunity to skate many great parks.
Although he started out at the Concrete Wave and
Skatopia, John was lured away by a park called
Wittier. This park was built in 1979 and had a much
more challenging terrain than the mid-1970s parks.
John would skate with his friend Richard Armijo, and
together the two would rage and terrorize and gener-
ally act like punks. Sure enough, the owner became
fed up with John and Richard's attitude. The two were
banned from the park.

This was a very harsh punishment for John — he
loved skateboarding and lived so close to the park.
He began showing up with Richard to ride on the
sidewalk outside the park. They would pretend they
were riding halfpipes and started to do the vert moves
(like aerials and handplants) on the street. Over time,
the pros inside the park (like Neil Blender) began
watching their crazy antics. At the time their moves
were completely different from anyone else's. This was
the genesis of modern-day street skating. One day,
Stacy Peralta came by the parking lot at the park. He
was so impressed with the guys' moves that he immediately offered to send the guys free boards.

Soon after, John started riding for a new park
called Skate City. He was thrilled to be on the team
and to skate for free. John started to enter more contests and began to move from sponsor to sponsor. At
one time or another John has ridden for G&S,
Variflex, Tracker, Zorlac and Gullwing.

John eventually started up his own company,
Lucero Skates. The board logo featured a red cross.
The idea for the logo came from John being hit by
cars while skateboarding and being carried off in an
ambulance. Although his company did enjoy a fairly
popular following, John achieved even greater success
with his other company, Black Label.

Kevin Harris

Kevin Harris was an exceptionally talented freestyler from Vancouver, British Columbia. He was one of the three freestylers sponsored by Powell Peralta. His flawless routines featured extremely smooth footwork. In the mid-1980s Kevin started his own skateboard distribution business, called Ultimate. It has become one of the largest skater-owned and -operated companies in the world. Kevin also owned and operated the world-renowned Richmond Skate Ranch. It was here where many of today's pros, like Colin McKay and Rob "Sluggo" Boyce, got their start.

Kevin Staab

Like many many skaters, Kevin started out on a Black Knight skateboard. In 1976, his father drove him to the Carlsbad skatepark. Kevin was so overwhelmed by Jay Adams skating the park, that it took him half an hour to enter the park. At the end of the decade he was fortunate to be able to skate with Tony Hawk. However, by the time he finished grade 8, his family moved out to Arizona. Despite the trip east, Kevin continued to skate and enter contests. He eventually found himself sponsored by Tracker Trucks and then Powell Peralta. From there, he got onto Sims. Besides being an excellent vert skater, Kevin was well known for his long blonde hair, wearing lots of pads and his friendship with members of the rock group The Cult. Over the years Kevin has enjoyed success with his own skate and clothing companies. He continues to skate vert and has become a mentor to upcoming vert legend Shaun White.

Before he took up skateboarding, Lance Mountain played in a bagpipe band as a drum major. Unfortunately, Lance was fairly small and he couldn't keep up the pace, so he was kicked out of the band. The band's loss was skateboarding's gain. In the fifth grade, Lance was given a skateboard by a friend and he started to progress from there. His father built him an eight-foot ramp and he began to work on his vert skills.

In 1978 Montabello skatepark opened and Lance made his first real money skateboarding ($15 for doing a safety promotional film for the park). He started to skate more backyard pools and his vert skating skills kept improving.

However, on one particular occasion, Lance took his parents to a place called "The Dustbowl" and things didn't go so well. He charged into his run and his parents found him a few minutes later in the deep end — knocked out cold! Lance was banned from skateboarding, but over time, he got back into it. In 1979, Lance took a trip to England with his father that energized his skateboarding. He visited lots of parks and Lance knew he was going to dedicate his life to the sport.

Returning from the UK, he entered his first major contest and got second place. After performing well at a number of ASPO (Association of Skate Park Owners) contests, he wound up being sponsored by Variflex. Things went well there for a time and Lance turned pro in 1982, just as skateboarding died. To supplement his almost non-existent pro income, he took a job at Variflex and learned about the internal workings of the skate industry.

Lance's mom talked to skate legend Stacy Peralta and asked him to give her son some advice about the industry. Stacy asked Lance to help him with the Bones Brigade. He left Variflex and joined up with Powell Peralta, assisting with the team. It would be almost two years before Lance got the chance to be a profes-sional skateboarder with his own signature board.

Lance's backyard halfpipe at his parents' place (called Mountain Manor) was the scene of many insane skate sessions. A lot of these were captured on the Powell Peralta videos, and Lance's part in the videos cata-pulted him to fame.

In 1985 Lance got married and had a child with his long-time girlfriend Yvette Loveless. In fact, Lance Junior has become quite a talented skater and appears with his father in print ads for Adidas shoes.

By 1991, the skate world had changed. Stacy had left Powell Peralta and Lance was expected to take over his posi-tion. Lance didn't feel comfort-able with this, and as a Christian, he had serious misgiv-ings about the direction being taken by companies like the notorious World Industries. He decided to start his own compa-ny called The Firm. Although it took time to develop, the compa-ny began to achieve success. Paralleling the career he had with the Powell Peralta videos, Lance continues to be extremely active in skate video. He is the feature presenter for the enor-mously popular skate video *411 Video* magazine.

91

Lester Kasai

Lester Kasai made a name for himself as an awesome vertical skater. His ability to pull off tricks that most people thought he would bail on increased his stature as a skate power. Oftentimes, he came close to hanging up on the coping of a halfpipe, but would pull the board in at the last moment. What many people might not know is that Lester was featured in *Transworld* in 1985 ollieing over a gap. This was one of the first gap photos ever captured. Lester teamed up with Adrian Demain to develop a brand called House of Kasai.

The saga of Mark "Gator" Rogowski begins in New York in 1967. At the age of three, Mark's parents divorced and he moved to San Diego with his mother and older brother. By the age of 10, he found himself consumed with skateboarding. He started winning contests and by 1982 won his first major title in Vancouver.

By the time the third skateboom hit in the mid-80s, "Gator" was right up there with vert superstars Tony Hawk and Christian Hosoi. He was an aggressive, brilliant vert skater with an immense following. His signature board for Vision sold incredibly well and at its peak hit 7,000 units per month. At $2.00 per board, Mark earned a cool $14,000 each month. But it didn't stop there — his clothing deal with Vision Street Wear earned him even more money.

Gator was all over the magazines and his touring escapades gained him a reputation as the wildest skater in the industry. He personified the word "icon." On tour in Arizona in 1987 he met up with two girls, Brandi and Jessica. There was an immediate attraction between Brandi and Gator. Within a few months, she left Arizona to live with him in California. The two had some pretty wild times — lots of partying and an appearance together in Tom Petty's "Freefallin'" video.

Although Gator was a vert superstar with legions of loyal fans, the skate world was changing towards the end of the 1980s. Street skating was in full bloom and vert was starting to be ignored. Gator was desperate to keep on top. In the fall of 1989, he went over to compete in West Germany. Here, his life took a dark turn at a skate party. Gator consumed way too much alcohol and fell out a second-story window, convinced he could fly. He impaled himself on a wrought-iron fence and had to undergo surgery in Germany. Back in San Diego he had plastic surgery in an attempt to salvage his modeling career.

Although Gator was beginning to look like his former self, mentally he had undergone a complete change after the accident. Gator told friends that he had found God. He gave up the booze, drugs and premarital sex. But Gator's fanaticism did not impress his girlfriend and she left him. This devastated the pro skater. Gator was angry and jealous that Brandi was seeing new people.

In 1991, Jessica, the other girl Gator had met in Arizona, found herself in San Diego and she looked Gator up, unaware that Brandi had fled to New York. The two met up and this was to have tragic consequences.

Jessica went missing. Foul play was suspected but the police had no leads. After a few months, Mark, racked by guilt, eventually contacted the police. He took them to the desert to show them her body in a shallow grave. Mark pleaded "no contest" and was sentenced to twenty-five years to life.

Mark "Gator" Rogowski

"I never thought that street skating would propel to this level."

Thrasher magazine, January 2001

Most skaters would say that Mark Gonzales embodies the term "skate legend." He has influenced millions of skaters around the world. Former and current pros rank him high on their own personal skate legends lists. It's easy to see why. "The Gonz" has always pushed himself. He has consistently brought skateboarding to new levels. Mark burst onto the pro circuit in 1985, riding for Vision. His board quickly became a bestseller. Well before most people had learned to ollie, Mark saw handrails as something to be ridden, not just to be used by cautious pedestrians.

In 1987, Mark pioneered new school kickflips and started the craze of writing words on grip tape. In 1989, Mark left Vision and started up his own company with Steve Rocco called Blind. ("Blind" is the opposite of "vision" — get it?)

Although there are many memorable moments in his (still unfolding) skate career, most skaters point to Steve's amazing video part in Blind's "Video Days." His flawless skating is highlighted by his ability to perform tricks "switch" (with his opposite foot forward). Oddly enough, after this triumphant video performance, Mark went into semi-retirement.

However, after a brief stint away from the limelight, Mark came roaring back. Mark is also an accomplished writer and has given readings of his published works around the world.

Mike McGill

Mike McGill grew up in Tampa, Florida, and started skating at the age of 12. Like most skaters, his room was plastered with pictures of the top pros of the time: Tony Alva, Jay Adams, Steve Olson and Stacy Peralta. "I used to stare at the posters and dream of skating the places those guys skated on a regular basis," he says.

After competing in local skatepark contests in Florida, Mike met up with Alan Gelfand and Tim Scroggs. Alan was the inventor of the ollie. Tim was one of the best freestylers at the time and a freestyle mentor to Rodney Mullen.

Mike, Alan and Tim joined together and formed an east coast team for Powell Peralta. The three skated in many amateur contests and traveled around the country performing demos. It didn't take long for Mike to turn pro and he came out with his own model in the early 1980s.

Mike's signature move, The McTwist, was born in a little town outside of Stockholm, Sweden, where Per Welinder grew up. Lance Mountain, Rodney Mullen and Mike were teaching skaters from all over Europe at a Swedish summer camp in 1984. It was the last week of the skate camp and Mike had done every trick he could think of at the time except one. As he explains, "I once saw a rollerskater named Fred Blood do a 540 flat spin at a skatepark in Cherry Hill, New Jersey, and thought, 'Man, that would be great to try on my skateboard.'"

About three years later at the very same camp, Mike dug up enough guts to commit to the first 360-degree turn and bail out to his knees. After about twenty or so tries he completed the final rotation making a complete one-and-a-half turns. "I couldn't believe it myself," he recalls. After making it a few more times it felt very natural for Mike. The skate world was amazed at the move and Mike's teammates, Rodney and Lance, named the trick "The McTwist."

In the early 1990s, Mike started up his own skate company, Chapter 7. Nowadays, he runs two retail shops that bear his name. Every time you see a skate or snowboard contest, chances are you'll see someone pull off a McTwist.

Mike Vallely

Hailing from New Jersey, Mike Vallely has a reputation for combining brains with brawn. He first gained recognition at a NSA contest in Oceanside in 1986 where he took first place in the amateur street division. Mike was the king of streetplants at the time. When he picked up his major sponsor, Powell Peralta, his career took off. Mike was featured in the "Public Domain" video and many skaters started to emulate his aggressive street style. In the early 1990s, Mike left Powell and joined up with Steve Rocco at World Industries.

Although Mike Vallely is known for his intense skating, he is equally known in the skate world for his writing. Mike has written poetry for some time and on many occasions has recited at contests. His writing is provocative and emotional and it strikes a chord with many of his fellow skaters.

Mike also reacts quickly when he sees a situation that he doesn't feel is going well. Most of these situations stem from interference by non-skateboarders at contests. Over the years, Mike has taken on a number of security guards.

Mike has been involved with a number of skate companies, including Television and Transit. However, he is achieving a great deal of success with John Lucero's Black Label company. In 2000, Mike ventured outside the world of skateboarding and started a part time career in pro wrestling.

No matter where Mike shows up — a skate contest or wrestling match — one thing is for sure: he will be raging.

Smith Mike

Mike Smith left a lasting mark on skateboarding — he was the inventor of the Smith grind. Mike's beginnings with the sport were skating barefoot at night carving down the hills of Hermosa. He met up with the Rocco brothers and got into freestyle. However, it was vert that beckoned and Mike charged into it.

In the early 1990s, Mike teamed up with World Industries and developed Liberty Skateboards.

Natas Kaupas

At the age of four, Natas Kaupas started skateboarding in an unusual way: He would lie down on his stomach and on his knees. It took him a while to progress to actually standing on the board, but once he could do that, he quickly moved to challenging terrain like banks. In the late 1970s Natas skated a few local skateparks, but he kept mainly to the streets.

When skateboarding died in the early 80s Natas kept skating and started to ride walls. He then progressed to handrails, which at the time were something skaters had only contemplated riding, but never really tried. At the start of skateboarding's third boom (around 1984), Natas got sponsored by Skip Engblom's skateboard company, Santa Monica Airlines. He was the only skater to ride for the company and his signature board was hugely popular.

Eventually, Santa Monica Airlines was picked up by Santa Cruz. In 1987, Santa Cruz released "Streets of Fire," one of the most memorable skate videos of all time. Natas blew a lot of people away with his incredible street skating. His ollies were insanely high for the time. Natas also helped to develop wall riding and railslides.

In 1990, Natas was the first skater to receive his own signature shoe (from Etnies). This was a fitting tribute to one of skateboarding's pioneers. Natas is still very active in skateboarding and currently rides for Element.

Neil Blender was one of the first pro skaters to combine his love of skateboarding with his passion for art. At Gordon and Smith, Neil designed his own unique graphics for his own signature model. His signature move was the Lien Air and he was famous for skating inside a house covered with plywood.

Although friends describe Neil's sense of humor as truly bizarre, his vert skating was brilliant. In the late 80s, he moved to Ohio to work with Alien Workshop and created dozens of eye-catching graphics.

Neil Blender

99

Per Welinder

Hailing from Sweden, it took Per only 18 months to be profiled in "Who's Hot" in *SkateBoarder*. In the early part of his skate career, Per was known for his freestyle prowess, including handstand kickflips. He eventually joined up with Powell Peralta and helped millions discover the joy of streetstyle skateboarding. In 1992, he partnered with Tony Hawk to create Birdhouse Projects, which has become a very successful skate company.

Pierre André

Pierre Andre is probably the only skater in the world who was allowed practice time while he was enlisted in the French army. Pierre was a world-class freestyler who moved into streetstyle towards the end of the decade.

Pierre did well in both European and North American contests. After Pierre left the pro ranks, he started working for a French skate shoe manufacturer called Etnies. Over the past decade, Pierre has grown this business into one of the largest skate shoe companies in the world.

101

Rob Roskopp

Born in Detroit, Michigan, Rob Roskopp was a very popular street skater in the 1980s. Rob started skating in 1975 at the age of twelve. He was fortunate to move to Cincinnati, Ohio, with his family. There, Rob was only two hours away from the world-renowned Apple skatepark. He skated it constantly. When the park closed, Rob began ramp riding and his skating quickly improved. He got sponsored by Madrid but found that skating was dying in Ohio. Rob moved out to California and within two weeks got a sponsorship from Santa Cruz. Within three months he turned pro.

Rob's pro model had one of the most interesting graphics — it featured a bullseye and then as new models were released, a monster slowly emerged.

Sergie Ventura

Big air. That's what makes Sergie Ventura a skate legend. He ruled the Mount Trashmore ramp at Virginia Beach. Sergie was one of very few vert skaters who successfully made the transition from the 80s to the 90s.

Rodney Mullen

Rodney Mullen's influence on skateboarding is now entering its third decade. It is pretty well impossible to imagine what street skating would be like now without Rodney's brilliant contributions. The list of tricks he has invented is endless. Suffice to say, it was about 20 years ago (circa 1982) that he invented ollie kickflips — one of modern-day skateboarding's most important tricks.

Rodney was born in Florida and when skateboarding hit big in the mid-1970s, he was anxious to start riding. His parents had other ideas. His father had turned down his requests numerous times and on New Year's Eve, 1976, Rodney asked again for a skateboard. This time, his father agreed, on the condition that Rodney wear full pads and if he had just one injury, he had to quit.

The very next day, Rodney and his father trekked down to the local mall and picked up a Banzai aluminum board. He started practicing freestyle tricks and within nine months he had his first sponsor: The Inland Surf Shop.

Rodney kept practicing and in due course, started winning many contests in his home state. In fact, after a little more than year of skating, Rodney impressed many of the California skaters who came out to compete at the Kona contest in 1978. By 1979, Rodney took top place at the pres-tigious Oceanside contest and was quickly sponsored by Walker.

Despite his great success, his father was urging Rodney to take up another sport. He figured Rodney had mastered skateboarding; now it was time to try golf. Fortunately for the skate world, Rodney stuck with skateboarding and kept training even harder.

At the age of 13, word of Rodney's incredible skills had reached Stacy Peralta. Stacy called Rodney and personally invited him out to a contest in San Diego. In Rodney's mind, this was to be his last competition with skateboarding. Rodney competed against freestyle champion Steve Rocco. Steve and Rodney battled it out and the contest was extremely close. Eventually, Rodney won and he officially started riding for Powell Peralta. As a result of this success, Rodney's father was motivated to keep him in skateboarding!

During the quiet early 1980s, Rodney kept perfecting his moves. He kept winning almost every contest he entered. As skateboarding started to become more popular in the mid-1980s, Rodney's fame grew. His astounding footwork in the Powell Peralta videos assured him of skate legend status immediately. In fact, his footwork is so technically blazing on these videos that even to this day, many viewers still can't comprehend what he is doing.

From the mid-80s to the beginning of the new decade, Rodney led the freestyle charge. Many tried to emulate his style, but few came even remotely close. Sadly, even though he was dominating the competition, he felt somewhat empty inside. "Each time I thought I got somewhere else, I realized that I hadn't gone anywhere."

Although it took some time, Rodney eventually put away his freestyle deck and moved towards the world of new school skating. He was encouraged by Plan B's Mike Ternasky and World Industries chief Steve Rocco. In 1992, Plan B's Questionable video came out and Rodney's blending of old and new moves showcased his incredible talents.

Throughout the 1990s Rodney's influence on skateboarding kept growing. He has gained a great reputation as a key innovator. This reputation spans not only tricks but board shapes and truck and wheel development. Towards the end of the 1990s, Rodney's life seemed to speed up even more. Among the many things he accomplished was appearing in two videos facing off against Daewon Song, creating the A-Team, developing Tensor Trucks and helping with the start-up of Enjoi Skateboards. It's obvious that it will be decades before Rodney's contribution to skateboarding can be fully documented.

Ray Barbee was a truly creative skater who built on the foundation of the streetstyle moves first done by people like Tommy Guerrero. He was able to develop more technical moves and this propelled skateboarding to even greater levels.

Ray credits his friend Robert Torrez with pushing him to follow skateboarding. The two would enter contests together, and they started to place in the top ten. Robert kept calling Steve Rocco, who worked at Sims/Venture. The two started to get product and were thrilled when eventually they wound up riding for Alva. From here, Robert and Ray went over to G&S but they were unhappy because the company wasn't helping them get to contests. Team manager Stacy Peralta (of Powell Peralta) had been following Ray's career for some time. When he asked Ray if he wanted to ride for the Powell Peralta team, Ray immediately said yes. He stayed with Powell Peralta for three years. He left to join The Firm, a new company that was created by his fellow teammate, Lance Mountain.

Ray Barbee

Freedom discovers a skater the moment he loses concern over what impression he is making or about to make.

—Powell Team Zine, 1999

Steve Caballero has over two decades of pro skating under his belt and shows no sign of stopping. Steve has left his mark both on vert and street skating for two generations of skaters. Known as "Cab", Steve has created many tricks, including "Caballerials."

His start with skateboarding was quite humble. Steve's mom would drive him to Winchester skatepark only once a week, since the family was short on money. But he'd get the maximum amount of time in his allotted skate day — he'd arrive first and leave last.

Steve had a drive to progress quickly, and he did just that. By 1979, he had become one of the hottest amateurs in California. A few months later he was at a contest and Stacy Peralta asked Steve to join his new skate team — the Bones Brigade. Steve was the first member and was soon joined by Alan Gelfand, Mike McGill and eventually people like Tony Hawk and Lance Mountain.

Steve credits Stacy for taking good care of him during his years on the team. In the early 1980s, Steve's talents exploded. He perfected the fakie 360 ollie (aka the Caballerial), along with moves like invert varials and lipside Smith grinds. Besides impressing people on a board, Steve received a lot of praise for his work on his fanzine, *Skate Punk Mag.* He also fronted his own punk band, The Faction.

Steve turned pro in 1981 and started earning $300 to $500 a month. By 1987, he was earning $12,000 to $16,000 a month. He was careful with his money and he never let it go to his head. In 1990, he was one of the first skate pros to get his own shoe model.

Steve Caballero

At the start of the 1990s, the key Bones Brigade members decided to strike out on their own and start their own companies. Steve did have thoughts of leaving, but decided to stick with Powell. He was quite shocked when Stacy Peralta left the company, but accepted it and carried on. Steve got involved with team management and promotion. His career continues to flourish at Powell and his skating abilities are still very strong. Not content to be known just as a vert skater, Steve has mastered many new school moves and can railslide with the best of them!

In today's environment, pro skaters jump from sponsor to sponsor frequently. It's a testament to Steve Caballero's integrity and ability that he has stayed with the same sponsor for over 20 years.

Steve Rocco

Steve Rocco is one of the very few skaters who have had an enormous impact in both the act of skateboarding and the business of skateboarding. Although his story starts out like most skaters', his journey has been decidedly different.

When Steve turned eleven, he received a skateboard from his father. He would skate with his brother Sal and eventually Steve landed on the Tunnel team in the mid-1970s. From there he got a sponsorship with Magnum (a division of Mattel). Steve's skill was to take vert moves and apply them to the street. At the time, most people thought he was crazy; in hindsight, he was years ahead of everyone. Steve knew instinctively that street skating was key to the development of skateboarding. In an interview with *Transworld* in 1988, the magazine asked about his unique riding:

TW: Did people used to laugh at you when you would street skate like that?
Steve: I used to get so much sh--t it wasn't even funny. "Why even bother doing it? Why don't you just go do it in a real environment like a pool? Why are you wasting your time in the streets?"

Although Steve spent time with Powell Peralta, he is best known in the mid-80s for being sponsored by Sims/Vision. In 1987 Steve was kicked off the Vision team and after meeting with Skip Engblom and Natas Kaupas, a decision was made to start up a company. Steve bought $6,000 worth of boards, borrowed $20,000 from a bookie and created a new skate company called World Industries.

Steve broke just about every rule in the book developing this company. He paid skaters double the royalty rate. Steve changed graphics from skulls and gore to cartoons. He took out advertising that was highly inflammatory against other skate companies and mesmerized the industry as a whole with brilliant, off-the-wall ideas. Steve was instrumental in creating a new era in the skateboard business. He went after the big five skate manufacturers and shook them to their very foundations.

By taking such an aggressive stance, World Industries paved the way for countless others. Practically nothing fazed Steve, and his sheer determination to shake things up was bordering on unbelievable. When *Transworld Skateboarding* refused to run one of his ads featuring a skater committing suicide because he couldn't land a trick, Steve was extremely angry. Instead of moving on and creating a different ad, Steve started up his own magazine called *Big Brother*.

Steve worked with many pros to create new skate companies within World Industries. (Plan B, 101, Blind). No matter how outrageous the idea, Steve was usually up for it. Not everyone appreciated his sense of humor and over the years, Steve has run into some resistance. However, gradually, Steve grew the company to a multi-million-dollar enterprise.

From street innovations to skate business innovations, Steve Rocco's efforts will continue to have repercussions for years to come.

Tommy Guerrero

In 1983, Tommy Guerrero entered the first-ever professional street contest. It was held in San Francisco's Golden Gate Park. Tommy took first place in the amateur division and his skate career took off from there. Tommy was the first street skater to get sponsored by Powell Peralta. This was an exceptional feat considering that, at the time, the team was mainly focused on vert riders.

In 1985 Tommy helped to change the face of street skateboarding forever. It was his amazing performance in the Bones Brigade's "Future Primitive" video that launched a billion ollies. Tommy can be seen ripping up the streets of San Francisco. In one particularly famous part, Tommy ollies over a driveway partition. It was a pivotal moment in the history of skateboarding and it started a revolution. Soon skaters everywhere were practicing their ollies and leaping over obstacles.

Eventually, Tommy left Powell Peralta and started up Real Skateboards, which was a very successful venture. He still skates and now records his own CDs.

In the late 1970s, *SkateBoarder* magazine profiled the skate scene in Sweden, and one of the key skaters featured was Tony Magnusson. He was a vert legend in his home country, and when he visited California in 1980 for three months, his reputation grew even larger. Tony has a natural skating ability and he packs a tremendous amount of power when he rides. In the early 1980s Tony was sponsored by Uncle Wiggly and became part owner in the company. He designed his own graphics and got involved in developing the concaves and shapes of the boards. After a few years, he launched his own company, Magnusson Designs, which achieved quite a high level of success. But Tony went on to even greater heights with H-Street (a company he created with Mike Ternasky). H Street was one of the first skater-owned companies to challenge the big five skateboard companies in the late 80s. While H Street was very successful, Tony had disagreements with his business partner. He eventually left and started up Evol. From here, he launched Osiris shoes, where he is the President and CEO.

Tony Magnusson

Jason Jessee

"Never say die." That pretty well describes the skate legacy of Jason Jessee. In profiling Jason in *SkateBoarder*, writer Thomas Campbell described his skating as "punk as f__k." Jason picked up skating at the age of thirteen and within a year was sponsored by Uncle Wiggly. He then rode for Vision until he decided to leave. After Vision, he wound up on Santa Cruz where he achieved major notoriety. One of the most popular skate videos of the 1980s was "Streets of Fire." Jason was cast as the lead character who is put in jail for the crime of skateboarding. Eventually, Jason left Santa Cruz and joined up with Consolidated.

There are many tales surrounding Jason, including the time he entered a contest at Del Mar with a broken arm. But it is for his vert moves, like massively high airs to fakie and revert tricks, along with his tattoos, that he is known best.

Hugh "Bod" Boyle

Hailing from London, England, Hugh got into ramp skating after watching a demo featuring Billy Ruff and Neil Blender at the Crystal Palace skatepark. The demo took place in 1983 and three years later Bod traveled to California. He toured a number of skate spots, then returned to the UK six months later. Bod did well in several major competitions (including a first place at the European Championships) and he found himself with two major sponsors: G&S and Thunder.

Marty "Jinx" Jiminez

Originally from California, Marty moved out to Ohio with his family. He hooked up with Bill Danforth and Rob Roskopp and together they were the founding members of the Middle Eastern Skateboard Series. (MESS). In 1983, Marty moved back to California. He was sponsored by both Madrid and Tracker Trucks. As a talented graphic artist, Marty wound up working for Brad Dorfman's company, Vision Skateboards. Marty was a very creative skater who did a lot of moves that few skaters could do. When Vision brought out his own signature model, it was a best seller.

Monty Nolder

A New Jersey native, Tom was fortunate to live near the Cherry Hill skatepark. His father was extremely supportive of his skating. Not only did Tom have a Firestone Flexiglass Ramp in his backyard, but his dad would also organize skatepark road trips.

In 1983 Tom moved to California and turned pro. He was a key innovator of many lip-tricks and was known for his aggressive riding.

Monty Nolder grew up in Florida and at the age of four he suffered an ear infection that caused him to lose his hearing. He made his first skateboard in high school. Although Monty's deafness did not hinder him in any way when he skated, there were a few occasions at contests when he'd do his routine and then find out it wasn't his turn. He'd wind up having to do the routine again.

The world-wide recession of the early 1990s hit the skateboarding business and it suffered its third fall. Thankfully, this crash was not as painful as the first two. From its ashes came a new style of skater and a new industry. Street skating became the only type of skateboarding featured in the magazines. New companies sprouted up overnight, along with hundreds of skate pros and many videographers waiting to preserve the moment.

With the introduction of the Extreme Games (now called the X Games) in 1995, the world got a chance to view skateboarding in a whole new light. By mid-decade, skateboarding had rebounded from the recession and once again exploded in popularity.

Nineties

As if television coverage, magazines and videos weren't enough to propel individual skaters to legendary status, a new medium was added to mix in the late 90s — the Tony Hawk's "Pro Skater" video game. Now moving into its third volume, this game allows players to choose their favorite skaters and perform their moves (at least in digital form).

Thanks to a change in the liability laws, many towns and cities were building skateparks once again. Vert skating also made a comeback, helped no doubt by its television-friendly presentation. The industry is now very healthy and the level of riding is reaching unprecedented heights. Although there are more skate pros now than there have been in the past, the competition is such that it takes a huge amount of effort to stay on top.

JAMIE THOMAS

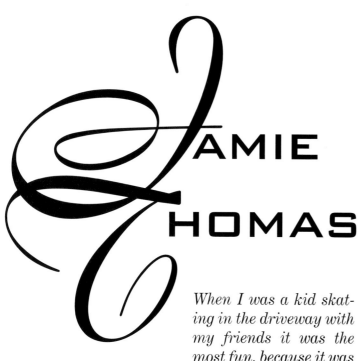

When I was a kid skating in the driveway with my friends it was the most fun, because it was so pure. Every once in a while I tap into that feeling. That's why I still skate. Skating is fun but it can come and go. God is forever!

Jamie Thomas's rise from skater to skate legend began the way many skaters gain their entry to the pro circuit — he sent "please sponsor me" videos out to prospective companies. In his native state of Alabama he worked in a skateshop and after sending out a number of his videos, Thunder Trucks and Spitfire wheels began sending him extra product for his use. This eventually led to a meeting with the Deluxe team manager (Deluxe being the owners of the Thunder and Spitfire) but Jamie still didn't make the team. But rather than give up, Jamie simply started sending a video each month for the next year and half — including one that featured him skating naked. ¶ Jamie finally got sponsored by Invisible (a division of Deluxe), but things didn't work out too well. He decided he needed to leave and wanted to ride for Plan B or Alien Workshop. Unfortunately, neither team was adding new people at the time. He then got a phone call from Ed Templeton, who was running his own company called Toy Machine (which was a part of the Foundation empire). Ed wanted Jamie to ride for Toy Machine and that's how Jamie began the next phase of his career. ¶ Although Jamie was passionate about skateboarding and was having success with Toy Machine, he felt he could offer the industry more. He approached Tod Swank, owner of Tum Yeto, about doing a clothing line called Zero. Tod was into the idea and Jamie started putting out t-shirts and sweatshirts. After about six months, Jamie decided he wanted to do boards — at the time he was still riding for Toy Machine. A business plan was put together and eventually Jamie left Toy Machine to ride for his own company — Zero. Jamie's notorious "leap of faith" in Zero's 1997 "Thrill of It All" video to this day still has the ability to freak people out. The leap was a two-story ollie over a rail at an apartment complex. The fact that he even attempted such a move was enough to attain skate legend status.

Bob Burnquist

Skateboarding has changed my life completely around from what I thought it would be, and it surprises me everyday.
—*Thrasher 1997*

As Brazil's most famous skate export, Bob Burnquist performs tricks on vert that many many skaters would have difficulty doing on flatland. His range of tricks and phenomenal ability are astonishing. Bob grew up in Brazil (his father is from the USA, mother Brazilian) and when his friend received a skateboard. Bob had to get one too. Bob's first sponsor was a clothing company called Moment Angular. He received free clothes and the owner would buy him a Coca Cola at the skatepark. He then started entering contests and getting more noticed. Bob's first real skate sponsor was a company called Slide which was based in Brazil. His next sponsor was a company called Urgh! Over time, Bob developed such an array of tricks that he felt comfortable to head over to the USA. He burst onto the international scene at the 1995 X Games in Rhode Island. Known for his incredible ability to do tricks switch, Bob has exerted a tremendous influence on vert and helped to bring about its popularity (with skaters and non-skaters alike).

Continuing on with the great tradition of vert pros having their own personal backyard ramps, Bob is the proud owner of a 64 foot wide vert ramp at his home in Vista, California. Bob rides for The Firm and eS shoes.

ANDY MACDONALD

Andy Macdonald had a fierce determination to be a skateboard super-star. It was a fire that burned so strong that it almost consumed him. Andy started skating in sixth grade on a Variflex board. He tried to keep up with his brother Kyle who was also obsessed. The two brothers would visit their father (Andy's parents got divorced the year he was born) in Michigan. Here their father set up a sketchy backyard halfpipe. Over at their mother's house, a quarterpipe was constructed. It was here where Andy established himself as a die hard skater — he was always the last guy to stop at each session.

Andy began travelling to skateparks and entering contests. By the age of 16, he had gained a fair amount of attention and even did a commercial for Fluff marshmallow spread. During the early to mid 1990s, vert skating died in popularity, but Andy was determined to make it. Against his mother's wishes, he drove out to California to try and get sponsored. Prior to arriving in San Diego, Andy had fired off a letter to friends and family. He also sent this letter to pro skaters he barely knew and skateboard compa

nies he wanted to ride for. Unfortunately, the letter was not well received by the majority of the skate world. They thought Andy was trying too hard to be accepted and it led to a great deal of misunderstanding about Andy within in the skate industry.

Andy found a number of odd jobs in San Diego and joined up with Mike McGill's company Chapter 7. However, things didn't work out well here and he was offered a chance to run Human Skateboards. Although Andy got his own model, he was living well below the poverty level. At the 1996 X-Games in Rhode Island

Andy won the vert contest against Tony Hawk. In 1997, he did well in a number of regular contests, but choked at that years X-Games, failing to make the cut. His father was there to offer support. Andy continued to press on and he eventually earned himself a spot on Powell. Andy is one of very few vert skaters to compete and do well in street contests and proba-bly the only skater in the world who've met a President of the United States — Andy met Bill Clinton in 1999.

STEVE BERRA

Steve was the first person to do a kickflip 50-50 down a handrail. This was back in 1995 in a Foundation video. Steve is one of the few street skaters with a vert background. He spent some time in Nebraska riding ramps. Over the years he's been sponsored by a number of companies. For a number of years he rode for Birdhouse Projects. In the fall of 2001 he joined the Alien Workshop team. Steve is also an actor and has appeared in a number of television shows, including *Nash Bridges* and *Felicity* (where he got hit by a bus!).

BUCKY LASEK

Born in Baltimore, Bucky has been skateboarding since 1985. Bucky got into skateboarding when his bike got stolen while he was shopping at a mall. He figured a skateboard would be a little more difficult to pinch. Bucky started on a Cabellero model that he received for Christmas. He began skating ditches and soon progressed to halfpipes. His first board sponsor was Skull Skates. At a Powell Peralta skate demo, Bucky was spotted by Tony Hawk and Stacy Peralta. They began sponsoring Bucky and eventually flew him out to California to film the video "Public Domain."

Bucky is noted for his ability to learn vert tricks very rapidly. When asked about how he accomplishes this, he told a *Transworld* interviewer that he works out moves on mini ramps and then pictures doing the trick in his mind. Bucky had a very good pro career with Powell Peralta but he left the company to join up with Birdhouse Projects (part owned by Tony Hawk). At Birdhouse he has racked up many wins, along with an impressive appearance in the Birdhouse video, "The End."

CHAD MUSKA

"The Muska," as he is known, has carved himself a legend among skate legends. Chad has a reputation as a skater who will try and skate just about anything. Born in 1977, he started skating in Arizona. He made his way to Las Vegas and eventually San Diego, where he lived well below the poverty line (Chad was practically homeless). Chad suffered a bad ankle injury that required metal pins but this did not deter him from his skating. He wound up being sponsored by Maple Skateboards. He then moved to Toy Machine but left over a dispute regarding his part in a video. He ended up on Shorty's and it is here that his career has blown up to incredible heights. ¶ Chad's signature model has been one of the biggest-selling decks over the past several years. Along with skating almost everything in sight, Chad finds time to pursue his love of hip hop. He owns his own music studio. He also runs his own shoe company, Circa, along with Ghetto Child Wheels. ¶ The proof of the Muska's popularity lies not only in product sales, but in his consistent placement in the top three of every reader poll for favorite skater.

TOM PENNY

Born in Dorchester, England, Tom Penny's exalted status has not been undercut by his elusiveness. His first sponsor was a skateshop in Oxford called SS20. Tom has a fondness for alcohol but for some reason, it has absolutely no effect on his skateboarding. In fact, it only adds to his mystique. Another factor is his tendency to drift in and out of the spotlight, causing fans to speculate about his whereabouts. Many consider Tom to be one of the greatest street skaters of all time. It is his low-key attitude that has kept him in the shadows. However, his skating has brought him international attention. Tom has ridden for Flip skateboards for a number of years.

CHRIS SENN

When he's not riding a skateboard, Chris Senn appears to be a pretty quiet guy. He keeps his distance and unlike many pros, doesn't get too wild. When he starts riding however, it's a different story. In contests, he is always the fastest skater on the course. At one time he was sponsored by Powell Peralta; nowadays he rides for Adrenalin. Chris married young and has one son.

HEATH KIRCHART

Although many skate legends have been sponsored by skating, clothing and shoe companies, it's doubtful anyone with the exception of Heath Kirchart has been sponsored by a newspaper. At the age of 13, Heath pulled a spectacular move at Carlsbad High School and got a Birdhouse sponsorship that very day. Profiled in *Transworld* at the age of 15, Heath was a paperboy for the *Orange County Register* who also happened to be an amazing street skater. He is credited with being the first to land a kickflip backside lipside on a handrail. Although he is featured quite often in skate magazines, Heath rarely gives interviews and when he does, his responses are quite brief. At one time Heath was sponsored by Foundation and was featured in three of their videos. However, he eventually got picked up by Birdhouse Projects, where he achieved great prominence as an all-around skater. His performances in two Birdhouse videos ("The End" and "Destroying America") have skaters dropping their jaws in response to his pyrotechnics and skate ability. In the fall of 2001 he left Birdhouse to skate for Alien Workshop.

DANNY WAINWRIGHT

When Reese Forbes hosted the Ollie Challenge at the Action Sport Retailer show in Long Beach, he probably thought that he had a good chance of winning. Britain's Danny Wainwright had other ideas. Danny's ollie was at 45.5" just over half an inch higher than Reese's.

Danny Way has fond memories of watching 80s skate legends like Gator, Hawk and Hosoi ride Del Mar skatepark. He witnessed the progress of mid-80s vert skating, never thinking that some day he would surpass the accomplishments of these riders.

Danny's father died at a young age and he was raised by his mother. He credits skateboarding for helping him endure a pretty difficult childhood. Danny took to skateboarding quickly and turned pro at age 14. A few people were pretty freaked out at Danny turning pro at such a young age. But he worked extremely hard to achieve his success and would practice at least three hours a day.

Danny's first sponsor was Vision. He then found himself riding with the Powell Peralta team. They asked him to join the team. Danny was featured in the 1988 video, "Public Domain" and his vert skating was a highlight of the tape. He was one of the first to do ollie blunts and half Cab blunts on vert. Unfortunately, things didn't seem to gel with Powell Peralta and Danny found himself working with Mike Ternasky of H-Street. He eventually became a pro for H-Street and starred in some breakthrough videos, including "Shackle Me Not." When Mike left H-Street to start Plan B, Danny went along with him.

In an interview with *Transworld* in October 1991, Danny was asked if had ever made a 900 (two-and-a-half rotations). He replied that he had landed the trick only three times. On August 3, 1997, Danny made vert history by jumping out a helicopter onto a halfpipe and blasting 16-and-a-half feet of air. Although he's known for vert skating, Danny is also an accomplished street skater. Among the companies he rides for are Alien Workshop, DC Shoes and Independent Trucks.

DANNY WAY

WILLY SANTOS

Willy Santos credits the Jackie Chan movie *Meals on Wheels* for getting him interested in skateboarding. "Little did I know," says Willy, "that I would be doing the funnest thing ever to me for a living."

Willy started to get coverage in skateboarding magazines and placed well in amateur contests. In 1991, he took first place at an NSA contest, which led to a sponsorship with Gordon & Smith. He was one of the first people on Birdhouse and his video part in "The End" is already a classic.

Willy is an incredibly consistent skater who rarely falls. And in what is surely a first for the skate world, Willy is part-owner in a haircutting salon/skate shop.

ERIC KOSTON

Born in Bangkok, Thailand, Eric Koston moved with his family to California at a young age. Eddie Elguera noticed Eric's skate talents and through his help, Eric got his career going. Thanks to Eddie, Eric wound up on the H-Street videos and getting his first sponsorship. From here H-Street evolved into Evol and Eric's video parts increased. He quickly established himself as one of the best technical skaters in the world, with an incredibly smooth style. Eric has perfected numerous tricks over the years, but he is best known for the Crooked Grind and the Fandangle (a one-footed Crooked Grind).

After Evol, Eric joined up with the World Industries empire and rode for 101 (a company owned by Natas Kaupas and Steve Rocco). After this, Eric left to start up Girl Skateboards with a number of former World Industry pros. He's also had tremendous success with Fourstar Clothing, and his Etnies signature shoe is a bestseller.

ETHAN FOWLER

Whether consciously or not, Ethan swiftly ollied his way into the spotlight at a mere sixteen years old and delivered a message: it's ok to be different. A message he's based a career on.
—*Transworld, December 1999*

There's no question Ethan Fowler has built a formidable career by standing out from the crowd. His part in the first Stereo Skateboards video in 1993 put him on the map and established him as a skater willing to depart from the norm. At the time, flip tricks were all the craze, along with enormously baggy pants and 37-millimeter wheels. Ethan brought something entirely different to the table and was a key player in helping to change the face of street skating. Ethan currently rides for Foundation Skateboards and Pig Wheels. Besides his incredible skating ability, he is known for dressing entirely in black (including socks).

GERSHON MOSELY

Riding my skateboard teaches me about life; it shows me what is real. —Transworld, March 2000

Gershon was born in 1974 in Compton California. At the age of 14, he started skateboarding. At the time, the sport was starting to die in popularity and eventually Gershon found himself alone with his skateboard. But he kept practicing and got his first sponsorship with Santa Cruz.

Over the years he's ridden for a number of teams, including Powell and the A-Team. He currently rides for Blind. Gershon has an amazing variety of tricks and is a very consistent skater.

GUY MARIANO

California native Guy Mariano got his first sponsorship with Powell. He then moved on to establish himself as a top pro at Blind and then Girl Skateboards. His most memorable video part was in Blind's "Video Days," where he can be seen street skating to the Jackson Five's "I Want You Back." Guy manages to keep a fairly low profile, but whenever he skates, he seems always able to pull off tricks that most people find inconceivable.

JASON DILL

Growing up in southern California in Costa Mesa, Jason Dill has been surrounded by skateboarding his entire life. He has memories of his mom buying him a marble-colored plastic skateboard when he was six years old. Jason was fortunate to be able to watch people like Ed Templeton skating in his neighborhood. By the time he was 10, Jason was already sponsored. He's ridden for a number of companies, including House of Kasai, Blockhead, 23 Skateboards and Black Label. However, at the moment he seems very content to be part of Alien Workshop. Besides having a reputation as a very talented street skater, Jason is also known for being very opinionated. But after seeing so much of the industry, that's no wonder!

JASON LEE

Jason Lee is one of the most gifted skaters I've ever met. —Rodney Mullen, Transworld profile, 1989

Jason Lee is one of the key skaters responsible for bridging the gap between the 1980s old school and the new street style era of the 1990s. His technical tricks and fluid style set the pace for a whole new generation of skaters. In eighth grade, Jason received a Variflex board and began grinding it on his driveway and doing boardslides on the curbs. His father couldn't understand why he was wrecking the graphics on his board. One of his first sponsors was Illusion Skateboards and Jason rode with Ron Chatman and Ed Templeton.

In 1988, Jason was featured in a photo sequence in *Transworld* doing a 360 kickflip. Although at the time this was thought of as more of a freestyle trick, it laid the foundation for streetstyle skating to become more technical. Jason was spotted skating at Hermosa Pier by Steve Rocco. Rocco put him on his SMA Rocco division team. This later became World Industries and Jason was eventually joined on the team by one of his major skate influences: Mark Gonzales. The Blind team set a new standard in street skating and "Video Days" still ranks as one of the best skate videos of all time.

In 1993 Jason left Blind and got together with Chris Pastras to start up Stereo skateboards. However, in 1995, Jason left skateboarding for Hollywood. He has acted in a number of films, including *Mallrats* and *Almost Famous*.

135

JEREMY WRAY

Jeremy Wray is known for big ollies over stairs and gaps. Born in Carmel, California, Jeremy moved around quite a bit, as his father was in the army. Jeremy's older brother Jaz was the first to take up skateboarding and he got Jeremy and his younger brother Jonas into it. The three brothers started making videos of themselves skating. Although they sent tapes out to lots of companies, no one seemed interested. When Jeremy and Jonas went to a skate camp they met up with Steve Ruge, the team manager for Spitfire and Thunder. Steve liked what he saw and began sending the brothers product. Shortly after this, Jeremy got on the Blockhead team. Jeremy is known as a perfectionist who will gladly put in overtime to ensure that a trick, graphic or video part is exactly the way he likes it.

Jeremy first gained attention in World Industries' "Rubbish Heap" video. In 1992 he left World Industries to ride for Birdhouse Projects. He is most commonly associated with Heath Kirchart and the two enjoy causing mayhem both on and off a skateboard. Whatever the obstacle — rails, police cars, video game terminals or blazing huts — Jeremy is there to ride it.

JEREMY
KLEIN

Ed Templeton's first skateboard memory is of rolling down a strip of sidewalk on a very skinny board from K-Mart. He stood with both feet together, toes facing forward towards the nose, his knees locked and hips gyrating in a slalom motion. "It was all about the curvy lines. It was the best going in circles over and over again," he recalls.

The skate world got its first real glimpse of Ed in 1988 in a Circle A Skateboards ad doing a 50-50 on a handrail. Unfortunately for Ed, they did not put his name in the ad. As the decade closed, Ed kept winning many amateur contests and started to receive a lot more magazine coverage. The decision to turn pro was pretty easy. "Skateshops were calling my sponsor at the New Deal. They were asking for an Ed Templeton pro board, so I turned pro," he says. As he recalls, "back then you had to really earn a board model. The companies needed assurance that your board would sell. It took a lot of contests and cover age to establish yourself as pro material."

So, in 1991, Ed got on the New Deal team, but two years later he left to start up his own company, Toy Machine. His company has been very successful. Ed is not only a very creative and accomplished street skater but a talented artist as well. His humorous and sometimes disturbing cartoons can be found in ads, on video boxes and of course as board graphics.

When asked about his favorite memories, Ed had this response: "There are so many memories. First and foremost, the opportunities skateboarding gave me to travel and see the world. That is priceless to me. Memories of winning my first pro contest in Munster, Germany, in 1990, the excitement and the mob of kids after my autograph. Being on tour across the US with Mike Vallely, criss-crossing the country with the Toy Machine team, and all the people who ever rode for me has been the best. Skating 7th Street school with Jeremy Klein back in the day, and my early skate days with best friend at the time, Jason Lee. These are but a few of the train of good memories I will hold forever."

ED
TEMPLETON

JOHN CARDIEL

John started skating in the mid-1980s and quickly progressed to become a Northern California legend. In 1993, he was awarded Skater of the Year from *Thrasher* magazine. Around the same time he could be seen in Lamar snowboard ads. John currently rides for Anti Hero boards and Spitfire wheels. He's known for fast and big tricks, and overall aggressive riding.

TIM BRAUCH

Although Tim Brauch died tragically in 1999 at the age of 25, he left a tremendous legacy to the world of skateboarding. He was a proud supporter of his hometown of San Jose and a great ambassador of the sport. Even though Tim was diagnosed at an early age with congenital heart disease, it never slowed him down. He started skating on his father's old board. He worked his way up through the amateur ranks and got a sponsorship deal with New Deal. At the age of 17, he turned pro for Santa Monica Airlines and eventually became part of the Santa Cruz team. As much as for his skating skills, Tim is remembered for his friendly, easy-going nature.

KRIS MARKOVICH

Skateboarding has given me the opportunity to do things I would have never imagined possible. If I can give back to skateboarding even half of what it's given to me I will be a happy man.

Kris is known for his speed and relentless determination. By the time he was 18, this native of Gulf Breeze, Florida, had been around the world twice, thanks to his skate skills. In pretty well every skate video he's been in, Kris has always managed to pull off an outstanding performance.

"My earliest memories of skateboarding are from the times when I knew I was hooked," Kris says. "I had always played baseball, football, basketball — all sorts of team sports when I was a kid. But when I got my first skateboard, that was the only thing that I could think about."

Kris is an all-around skate, comfortable on all types of street terrain. Throughout the years, he has been a member of a number of skate teams. However at the moment he rides for Element.

Matt Hensley started skating seriously around 1982. At the time he was in grade seven and having some troubles in school. He was hanging out with a pretty crazy group of kids. Although he didn't participate in what they were doing, Matt would be blamed for all kinds of things. For grade eight, Matt was sent to a naval academy. He experienced a great deal of harsh treatment at the academy, including getting kicked and punched by five guys at once and having to march ten hours straight. Thankfully, Matt survived this experience and kept practicing his skateboarding. ¶ He was working at a skateshop when Gale Webb came in. Gale ran a series of skate shows and asked Matt to join in. He skated with Danny Way (who lived nearby) and the two wound up doing a large number of demos for Gale. At one of them, Everett Rosencrans from Vision spotted Matt. Everett was impressed enough with Matt's abilities to offer him free product right there at the demo. Sadly, the opportunity for free Vision product was not all it was cracked up to be. Matt was shipped one complete board and then nothing else for an entire year. Finally, at a contest in Las Vegas, Matt placed in the top five and secured himself a solid sponsorship deal with Vision. ¶ From Vision, Matt moved to H-Street. It was here that he gained a reputation as a phenomenal street skater. In 1988 he was laying the foundation for a generation of new street skaters. His influence was profound and his technical skating was studied by millions of skaters worldwide. In 1992 Matt went into semi-retirement. Towards the end of the 1990s he came back and he now rides for Black Label.

MATT HENSLEY

142

A San Francisco native, Mike Carroll's first memories of skateboarding are of riding on his cousin's board. Pushed by his brother and cousin, Mike didn't know how to stop, so he would wind up crashing into curbs or garbage cans. From this humble beginning, Mike has gone on to make a huge mark. Mike was sponsored by H-Street and at the age of 14 turned pro. He was instrumental in the start-up of Plan B. In the 1992 "Questionable" video, Mike tears up San Francisco's Embarcadero skate spot. In 1993, Mike left the World Industries fold and started up Girl Skateboards along with Rick Howard. Many believe that Rick is one of the most progressive riders to ever grace skateboarding. He's a very technical skater and thinker. Mike used to add parts to his skate shoes to make them function better. This led him to start Lakai Shoes with Rick Howard.

MIKE CARROLL

OMAR HASSAN

Originally hailing from Yemen, Omar Hassan got into skateboarding via his older brother. Omar is one of a few select riders who made the crossover from vert to street skating. He is an accomplished vert rider who can handle rail tricks without a problem. Omar currently rides for Black Label and has his own pro model shoe from Vans.

PAT DUFFY

"Pat opened the doors for everybody"
—Matt Mumford, On Skateboarding
video magazine, 2000

It took only one video part for Pat Duffy to
explode onto the skate scene. In 1992's
"Questionable" video from Plan B, Pat 50-
50'd a double-kinked rail of exceptional
length. Many skaters still talk about this
trick to this day. The video also captured
Pat doing a rail slide in the rain.
Pat began skateboarding in 1985 but he
admitted in an interview with Thrasher
that he didn't really get serious about it
until 1989. He rode for H-Street for about
three months, then joined up with Mike
Ternasky at Plan B. Pat has had a profound influence on skateboarding and
has constantly pushed the envelope.
Besides his rail abilities, Pat is known for his
backside grinds. He currently rides for
Think Skateboards.

RICK McCRANK

Born in Peterborough, Ontario, Rick McCrank got into skateboarding via his brother. He started at the age of 12 and found himself hooked on the sport. Over the past few years, Rick has performed exceptionally well at street competitions all over the world. He has made a name for himself as a very smooth and consistent skateboarder. Rick currently rides for Girl Skateboards and his own wheel company, Momentum. Rick is also really into natural foods — he co-owns an herbal remedy company and is a vegan.

DAEWON SONG

Born in Seoul, Korea, Daewon moved to Hawaii at the age of two and a half. From here he moved to California. In 1988, at the age of 13, Daewon discovered skateboarding. By the time the early 90s hit, Daewon had turned into a super technical skater. He first came to the skate world's attention in the second World Industries video. Team manager and part-owner Rodney Mullen was impressed with his style and brought Daewon onto the team. His appearance in "New World Order" (released in 1993) features astounding technical footwork, like fakie 360 flip noseblunt slides. Daewon's insane footwork off of picnic tables and high-risk ollies over roof gaps has mystified and enthralled skaters worldwide. He currently runs his own board company, Deca.

ROB DYRDEK

Since 1990, Ohio native Rob Dyrdek has ridden for Alien Workshop. He is one of skateboarding's most consistent and technical riders. Rob is a very smooth and stylish skater and he's known for his ability to escape getting hurt when bailing. Rob also started his own record label, called PJ's. He also rides for the DC Shoe Company.

RICK HOWARD

Canadian Rick Howard's earliest skate memory is of losing his front tooth due to speed wobbles on a hill. When Rick was asked what events led him to turn pro, he replied, "I clicked my heels and said 'Please let me be pro, please let me be pro,' just like Dorothy in the *Wizard of Oz.*"

Rick has a very smooth style and lots of Canadian pride. He rides for Girl Skateboards and recently joined up with the Lakai skate shoe company.

SEAN SHEFFEY

Sean Sheffey first got attention in a Life Skateboards video. He is a talented street skater who will try anything once. He was an early proponent of shove-its, ollie gaps, double-kinked rails and tricks on picnic tables. Sean has some notorious stories surrounding his life, some of which border on mythical.

BAM MARGERA

Not one to take himself too seriously, Bam Margera grew up in Pennsylvania. He's gained a huge following for his insane antics both on and off a board. Bam is best known for his CKY videos, along with being a co-star of MTV's *Jackass* program. They showcased him in a variety of absolutely crazy situations, most of which are unprintable. Bam is a hard core street skater. His signature move is a switch stance backside tailslide. On the most recent Tony Hawk Gigantic Skatepark Tour, Bam jumped out of a six-story window into a swimming pool. His current sponsors include Element, Volcom, Spitfire and Adio shoes.

BRIAN ANDERSON

The youngest of 14 children, Brian has made a name for himself both in North America and Europe. He has won the Munster, Germany, skateboard contest twice. A very solid, technical skater who makes even the most difficult tricks look easy, Brian used to ride for Toy Machine, which was also his first sponsor. In 1999 he was voted by sponsored riders as the best street skater for the Transworld Skateboarding Magazine Awards. He now rides for Girl Skateboards.

ELISSA STEAMER

Hailing from Fort Meyers, Florida, Elissa Steamer has left many male skaters in the dust. She is an intense, aggressive skater who is not scared to attack rails, ramps or whatever else is in her path. Riding for Toy Machine, Elissa is an inspiration to both female and male skaters everywhere.

GEOFF ROWLEY

Born in England, Geoff Rowley has quickly risen through the pro ranks. Geoff dominates the street skating scene with his fast, aggressive skating. He is known as a perfectionist but more important, he is willing to try anything. This includes going full speed into rails that most skaters wouldn't dream of touching. In February 2001, he was named Skater of the Year by *Thrasher* magazine. Geoff has been a pro rider for Flip Skateboards for a number of years, as well as for Vans Shoes.

CHET THOMAS

COLIN McKAY

Chet Thomas started skating at the age of 11 and by the time he was 12 had a sponsorship with Powell Peralta. In 1988, he was featured in a montage in the "Public Domain" video (along with other "rubber boys" Steve Saiz, Ray Barbee and Eric Sanderson). At the age of 18, Chet turned pro to ride for New School, followed by stints at various manufacturers, including Santa Cruz, Platinum and the A-Team.

In 1997, Chet got into the wheel-manufacturing business. Starting up in his garage, Chet has achieved a great deal of success with Darkstar Urethane. Chet is also a partner in two skate shops called Aftermath. Chet has a reputation for being an extremely technical skater. His signature moves are a wide range of variations of a hard flip.

Canadian Colin McKay was destined to be a skate legend: At the age of 11, he got the table of contents page in *Thrasher* magazine and two years later he was featured in *Transworld* in the "Check Out" section. Colin's rise to vert fame was due primarily to his sessions at former Powell pro Kevin Harris's Richmond, BC, Skate Ranch. In 1992 he was featured in the "Questionable" video and his vert and street parts are exceptional. From Plan B, Colin moved over to Girl Skateboards. He is also active in the business side of skateboarding — he is part-owner of two skateshops called RDS (Red Dragon Supply).

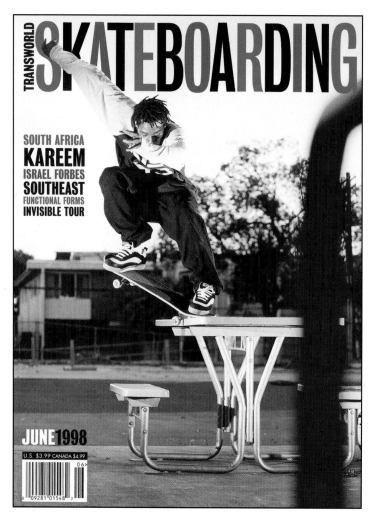

TRANSWORLD SKATEBOARDING

SOUTH AFRICA
KAREEM
ISRAEL FORBES
SOUTHEAST
FUNCTIONAL FORMS
INVISIBLE TOUR

JUNE 1998

U.S. $3.99 CANADA $4.99

0 09281 01548 2   06>

KAREEM CAMPBELL

Kareem was born in Harlem, New York, but at an early age spent a considerable amount of time in Los Angeles. He is one of the few pros who started skateboarding at a very late age — 16. Kareem comes from a pretty tough background. He comes from the streets and has been involved with some heavy stuff. However, skateboarding has carried him to great heights. Kareem was greatly affected by watching Ray Barbee in a Powell Peralta video, and this pushed him even harder to pursue skateboarding excellence. ¶ He got his first sponsorship with SMA/World Industries. At the age of 19, Kareem turned pro. Over the course of a skate tour, things turned ugly on the road and Kareem and Jason Lee left World Industries to form a company called Blue. The company only lasted a year and Kareem eventually returned to World. He started up two companies with World — one was a shoe company called Axion and the other was a board/wheel company called All City. He recently left the World Industries fold and started up his own distribution company, KSL.

ROB {SLUGGO} BOYCE

Hailing from Canada, Rob grew up at the Richmond Skate Ranch in British Columbia. He is a vert master and was the first skater ever to do a front flip on a board. "Sluggo" is also one of the few skate pros to be a pro snowboarder. He has ridden for World Industries for many years (on both teams). Rob got his nickname because people thought he looked similar to the cartoon character. He also has done professional stunt work in movies.

MARC JOHNSON

Marc Johnson combines superb technical skating ability with massive style. He takes a low-key approach to his skating and is very humble about his amazing abilities. In the late 90s Marc joined up with the A-Team, a technical juggernaut of skaters. After its demise, Marc started up Enjoi, which is part of the World Industries family.

ANDREW REYNOLDS

Andrew grew up in Florida and started skateboarding at the age of 12. As a young teenager, he caught the Birdhouse team in their "Ravers" video. Eventually Andrew wound up riding for Birdhouse. Andrew displays remarkable control with his skate and can pull huge frontside flips over stairs and rails. In 1999 (just eleven years after he started skating), Andrew won *Thrasher* magazine's Skater of the Year award. Andrew now rides for Baker Skateboards and hangs out with his skate buddies the Piss Drunx.

SAL BARBIER

Sal Barbier is an extremely stylish streetskater. A native of San Diego, Sean started riding pro for H-Street and then moved to Plan B. He had his own pro shoe with Etnies, which became very popular in the mid-90s. Sean now rides for Aesthetics and Elwood clothes.

Sal was the perfect roommate: super quiet and respectful. Then he started hanging out with Sean Sheffey.
—Former roommate and Fishlips president Perry Gladstone

RUNE GLIFBERG

Rune comes from Denmark and has established himself as among the very best vert skaters in the world. He's known for his powerful assortment of tricks and willingness to push his own limits. He is an awesome skater to watch. Rune is part of the European skate powerhouse that is Flip Skateboards.

SALMAN AGAH

Salman Agah is the pioneer of switchstance and helped to popularize it throughout the 1990s. His earliest skate memories involve being in Ocean City, Maryland, on the boardwalk, going into a skateshop for the first time around 1977. "I just remember being so excited as we walked in and I saw all the boards hanging from the ceiling," he recalls. "There was every kind imaginable, so it seemed. I remember repeating, 'I want one of the wide ones,' over and over to no avail." Salman ended up with the typical banana board but he doesn't remember riding it much, since his dad was always paranoid about Salman getting hurt and dirty. ¶ Unfortunately, Salman lost this board in a sewer and didn't get back into skating for quite some time. However, he eventually returned to the sport and by the late 1980s Salman was getting a lot of recognition for being very proficient at nollies. This naturally led to his ability to skate switch at a time when the way people skated was going through a lot of changes. Salman was one of the first skaters to begin doing switch tricks that were up to par with the tricks that regular-footed riders were doing. ¶ In 1991, Salman turned pro at a competition at the Olympic stadium in Barcelona, Spain. Salman credits his coverage in the mags, placing well in am contests and touring the U.S. and Europe with establishing himself as a pro rider for Real Skateboards In 1994 he won Skater of the Year in *Thrasher* magazine. He currently rides for Black Label and Vans. ¶ "I have so many fond memories of skateboarding over the years. Getting to skate with all my skateboarding heroes over the years has been pretty amazing. To also be able to travel all over the world has been quite a treat."

MIKE CRUM

Hailing from Texas, Mike Crum has fond memories of skating at the Skate Time skatepark in Dallas. Here he watched vert 80s legends Jeff Phillips and Craig Johnson and this set a course for him — vertical skating. One of his first sponsors was Zorlac (an infamous Texas skate company) and he turned pro at the age of 16. Unfortunately, his timing wasn't that great. Eight months after he turned pro, vert skating died in popularity. Street skating overtook vert and his paychecks dwindled to about $100 a month. He relied on fellow skaters to help him through this vert drought. Nowadays, Mike is there to help out other skaters who might need assistance.

INDEX

PHOTO CREDITS

The author and publishers wish to thank all those who contributed their words and pictures to this volume. Every effort has been made to give credit to the originators of materials used in this book. Any questions in this regard may be directed to the publisher.

Our sincere thanks to all photographers and archivists who helped document the skate legends found within this book.

Adams, Bruce (GBJ/Lapper Magazine)
Chris Miller
Jeff Phillips

Atiba (Transworld cover)
Kareem Campbell

Blake, Mike
Mark Rogowski

Bowman, Brad
Monty Nolder

Cooper, Lynn
Pierre Andre
Steve Cabellero
Kevin Harris
Christian Hosoi
John Lucero
Lester Kasai
Tony Magnusson
Chris Strople

Doubt, Dylan
Geoff Rowley

Goodrich, Jim
Jay Adams (Back Cover)
Mickey Alba
Steve Alba
Tony Alva
Dave Andrecht
Neil Blender
Eddie Elguera
Alan Gelfand
Paul Hackett
Steve Olson
Shogo Kubo
George Orton
Duane Peters
Bobby Piercy
Lonnie Toft

Gregory, James Alexander
Danny Bearer

Little, Monty
Tom Sims

Miyoda, Glen
Jay Adams
Bob Biniak
Brad Bowman
Rene Carrasco
Richy Carrasco
Steve Cathey
Dave Hackett
Henry Hester
Skitch Hitchcock
Russ Howell
Tom Inouye
Ray "Bones" Rodriguez
Doug "Pineapple" Saladino
Dale Smith
Bob Skoldberg
Gayle Webb
Mike Weed
Vicki Vickers
Stacy Peralta

McCourt, Mike
Pat Duffy
Eric Koston
Sean Sheffey

Mitchell, Dan
Rob "Sluggo" Boyce
John Cardiel
Bob Burnquist

Morris, Jody
Mike Vallely

Needam, Scott
Bill Danforth

Segovia, Patty
Cara Beth Burnside
Tony Hawk
Kevin Staab

Serfas, Scott
Mike Crum
Rick McCrank
Chet Thomas
Jeremy Wray

Sohar, Brandon
Tim Brauch
Bob Burnquist
Mark Gonzales
Rune Glifberg
Gershon Mosely

Starr, Scott
Eddie Reategui
Waldo Autry
Sal Barbier
Tony Hawk (cover)
Christian Hosoi
John Hutson
Jason Lee
Mike McGill
Guy Mariano
Chad Muska
Ty Page
Tommy Guerrero

From the Collection of Dale Smith
Brad "Squeak" Blank
Harry "Skip" Frye
Mike Hynson
Phil Edwards
Brandon "Woody" Woodward
Joey Cabell
John Freis
Mickey Maga
Bernard "Midget" Farrelly

Vuckovich, Miki
Bod Boyle
Frankie Hill
Omar Hassan
Jeff Kendall
Rob Roskopp
Billy Ruff
Ben Schroeder
Mike Smith

Ellen Oneal
Ellen Oneal

Alien Workshop
Jason Dill
Rob Dyrdek
Danny Way

Bahne
Dennis Shufeldt

Birdhouse
Steve Berra
Heath Kirchart
Bucky Lasek
Willy Santos
Jeremy Klein
Tony Hawk
Andrew Reynolds

Destructo Industries
Chris Senn

Duffs Shoes
Matt Hensley

Element
Natas Kaupas
Bam Margara

Este
Salman Agah

The Firm
Ray Barbee

Girl
Mike Carroll
Rick Howard

Gullwing
Jason Jessee

Independent
Jeff Grosso
Robert Valdez

Logan Earth Ski
Robin Logan

Matix Clothing
Marc Johnson
Rodney Mullen
Daewon Song (table of contents)

Powell
Danny Wainwright
Steve Cabellero

Red Bull Photofiles (Ulrich Grill)
Andy Macdonald
Colin Mckay
Sergie Ventura

Road Rider Wheels
Eric Dressen

SkateBoarder Magazine
Rick Blackhart
Steve Hilton
Torger Johnson
Laura Thornhill
Gregg Weaver

Sims
Steve Rocco

Swatch
Per Welinder

Tum Yeto
Brian Anderson
Ethan Fowler
Kris Markovitch
Elissa Steamer
Ed Templeton
Jamie Thomas

Vision
Tom Groholski
Marty "Jinx" Jiminez